Microsoft

Microsoft
Lync 2013 Plain & Simple

Darren Lloyd

Published with the authorization of Microsoft Corporation by:
O'Reilly Media, Inc.
1005 Gravenstein Highway North
Sebastopol, California 95472

ISBN: 978-0-7356-7461-5

1 2 3 4 5 6 7 8 9 TI 8 7 6 5 4 3

Printed and bound in Canada.

Microsoft Press books are available through booksellers and distributors worldwide. If you need support related to this book, email Microsoft Press Book Support at *mspinput@microsoft.com*. Please tell us what you think of this book at *http://www.microsoft.com/learning/booksurvey*.

Microsoft and the trademarks listed at *http://www.microsoft.com/about/legal/en/us/IntellectualProperty/Trademarks/ EN-US.aspx* are trademarks of the Microsoft group of companies. All other marks are property of their respective owners.

Acquisitions and Developmental Editor: Kenyon Brown
Production Editor: Kristen Borg
Editorial Production: Kim Scott
Technical Reviewer: Alex Lewis
Copyeditor: Bob Russell
Indexer: BIM Indexing Services
Cover Design: Twist Creative • Seattle
Cover Composition: Karen Montgomery
Illustrator: S4Carlisle Publishing Services

For Sharran.
What we have can only be described as "special."

Contents

14

Acknowledgments

The process of authoring this book has been an enjoyable and fulfilling experience, and the thought that its content will introduce readers to a revolutionary new way in which to work and communicate while dramatically improving their productivity is something that provides me with great satisfaction.

Of course, there are a number of people who have assisted me along the way, including the team at O'Reilly: Kenyon Brown, Kristen Borg, Bob Russell (at Octal Publishing, Inc.), and many more who worked "behind the scenes." I thank you all for all the invaluable help and guidance you have provided from the outset.

I also need to say a huge thank you to my colleague at Modality Systems, Alex Lewis, for doing a fantastic and accurate job as the technical editor of the book—while authoring his own book at the same time.

The journey to this point has been a long one, and indeed there are a number of individuals who have shown belief in me and offered good advice and encouragement throughout my career. You guys know who you are, and I thank you for the opportunities you have afforded me.

Finally, to my parents for giving me the determination and belief to succeed, and my wife, Sharran, for the encouragement and unwavering faith you have in me. I thank you all.

About this book

1

Microsoft *Lync 2013 Plain & Simple* is for users who want to use Lync to improve the way they communicate and collaborate within the workplace. This book demonstrates how the various modalities of Lync 2013 make it easy to seek out the availability of contacts and then select the best method by which to communicate with them. It also demonstrates the ease by which you can share content so that you can collaborate on a one-to-one basis or as part of a multiparty conference call.

Lync 2013 delivers features such as "presence," instant messaging, conferencing (audio, video, and web), collaboration, and enterprise voice to your desktop or mobile device, providing you with the tools that simplify the way you work and remove the frustrations associated with traditional methods of communication.

You can use this guide to set up a communication environment unique to your own requirements, and along the way, find new exciting ways in which Lync 2013 can improve your efficiency and productivity within the workplace.

In this section:

- Simplified communications
- A quick overview
- A few assumptions
- Adapting task procedures for touch-enabled devices
- Sign in and enjoy Lync 2013

Simplified communications

Ask any group of people who have experienced Lync 2013 whether they could work without it, and almost in unison their response would be a resounding "no." Having embraced their first exposure to unified communications with a little trepidation and the thought of another false IT dawn, Lync users soon see its intuitive interface as second nature and a natural common sense way by which to communicate. It's said that simple ideas are always the best.

Each user will employ Lync in a different way, setting up Lync environments in a manner that addresses their individual working requirements. Some will rave about the amount of time they've saved by taking advantage of "presence," both via the Lync client and also via core Microsoft applications such as Outlook, to check the availability of colleagues and coworkers instead of blind-calling them. Others will point to the Lync Online Meeting facility as the tool that has made them more productive, and that saves their company the costs traditionally associated with attending meetings such as travel and accommodations.

The cool thing about Lync is that it provides you, the user, with the power to dictate how best to set up and use your communication environment. With Lync, you can easily reach out to colleagues and contacts from wherever you chose to work, on a multitude of different devices, and in a way that will make you think, "However did I manage before I had Lync?"

A quick overview

This book has been written so as to provide you with all the information and skills you need to become a proficient user of Lync 2013, while at the same time making you more efficient and productive within your working environment. The book is filled with easy-to-follow, step-by-step tasks for every conceivable function that Lync provides. It's structured in such a way that you don't have to read through pages and pages before you get to the task for which you require assistance. Just look up the task, go directly to the specific section, and then put the book down until you need to reference it again.

Each section provides an overview of the tasks that you want to complete—for example, "Manage contacts" or "Start a conversation"—and then goes on to discuss those tasks in more detail.

Section 2 provides a brief overview of the changes you are likely to find in Lync. It highlights the changes to show how Lync 2013 looks and feels and also points to new features including *tabbed conversations* and *persistent chat*.

Section 3 gets you started. It introduces you to the login screen and then takes you through a journey of the main Lync 2013 interface, covering tasks such as changing your presence and adding a note to your status—elements that you will change frequently throughout the day.

Section 4 introduces you to contacts and, more specifically, how to search, add, delete, monitor, and categorize them within Lync. Managing your contacts is crucial to maintaining an environment that is easily navigable and provides effortless access to colleagues and coworkers.

Sections 5 and 6 focus on how to start communicating and collaborating with your contacts. These sections demonstrate everything from sending your first instant message, right through to sharing a document with a colleague on which you can both collaborate.

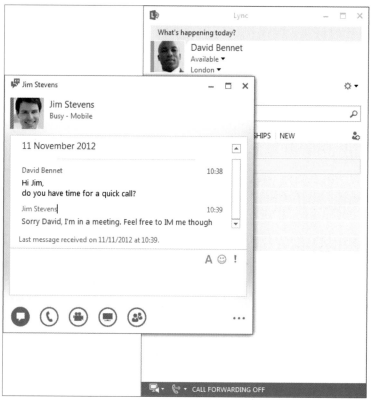

Section 7 provides an overview of tight integration that Lync 2013 has with Outlook. It highlights the presence of your contacts, and describes the various views and options available to you when using the functionality of Lync from within Outlook.

Sections 8 through 11 introduce you to the world of voice. Lync 2013 is a fully functional enterprise voice-capable platform; or, to stay in character with the nature of this book and keep it simple, you can make a receive telephone and video calls. These sections show you how easy it is to make calls, use voicemail, and do everything you would expect of a fully functional telephony system, such as call forwarding, transferring a call, placing callers on hold, changing your voicemail greeting, and activating simultaneous ringing.

Section 12 focuses purely on conferencing. This section demonstrates how to set up a conference call on the fly and how to schedule conference calls with internal and external contacts. It also demonstrates how to join a conference and how to set meeting options such as who can present material.

Section 13 introduces a new Lync 2013 feature called persistent chat. It provides an overview of how and why persistent chat rooms are used, demonstrates how to create them, and also shows you how you can receive automatic updates when new posts are added to chat rooms that you follow.

Section 14 is a guide to changing the Lync 2013 Options menu. I describe how each configurable element in your Lync environment is controlled and the various options that are available.

Appendix A is a reference that lists several useful keyboard shortcuts.

A few assumptions

In preparing this book I've made a few assumptions along the way about you as a user and about the applications and devices that you're using.

To keep things simple and to ensure that we're all starting from the same position, I've assumed that you are familiar with the basics of your computer; for example, how to turn it on, how to double-click your mouse, and so on.

I've further assumed that you have the standard Microsoft Lync 2013 client for Windows 8, that you're using the default settings, and that you have connectivity to your company's network and have access to audio and video devices. Finally, I've assumed that you are using Outlook 2007 or newer as an email client.

To sign in to Lync, you'll require a user name and password. These should have been provided to you by the administrator at your company, so if you don't have these credentials, contact your IT department to arrange to get them. After you have your own sign-in credentials, you'll be able to enjoy the many benefits of Lync 2013.

Adapting task procedures for touch-enabled devices

In this book, we provide instructions based on traditional keyboard and mouse input methods. If you're using Lync on a touch-enabled device, you might be giving commands by tapping, either by using your finger or with a stylus. If so, substitute a *tap* action any time I instruct you to *click* a user interface element. Also note that when I instruct you to enter information in Lync, you can do so by typing on a keyboard, tapping in the entry field under discussion to display and use the On-Screen Keyboard, or even speaking aloud, depending on how your computer is set up and your personal preferences.

Sign in and enjoy Lync 2013

I truly hope that you find this book helpful and that you too become one of those people who can't imagine working without Lync. When I started to write this guide, I did so in the belief that what it contains has the ability to change the way you work and communicate and that essentially it would make your working life easier, more straightforward, and ultimately more productive.

I hope you have as much fun using Lync as I had writing this book. So, go ahead; sign in and enjoy Microsoft Lync 2013!

What's new in Microsoft Lync 2013

2

Microsoft Lync 2013 is an enterprise-ready, unified-communication platform, or put in more simplistic terms, a platform with which you can improve the way you communicate with colleagues and coworkers (both within and outside your organization), while at the same time improving your productivity.

Lync 2013 provides you with the opportunity to tailor your communication environment to your individual requirements, and has been designed to enable you to interconnect and collaborate from wherever you might be, whether that's in the office, at home, or in your favorite coffee shop.

What's more, Lync also provides you with the ability to sign in to more than one device at a time, making it possible for you to use your desktop computer, Windows Surface, Windows Phone, and a Microsoft Lync Certified desk phone all at the same time.

Microsoft has introduced a number of fantastic new features in Lync 2013, and the most noticeable enhancements and improvements are discussed on the following pages.

A new user interface

Microsoft has introduced a few subtle changes to the look and feel of the Lync 2013 user interface, but overall, the functionality and navigation remains familiar when compared to previous versions. If you have experience with Lync 2010, you will have no trouble locating the functions you use regularly; if you are new to Lync, you will find it easy to use and navigate. Section 3, "Getting started with Lync 2013," covers the Lync 2013 interface in more detail.

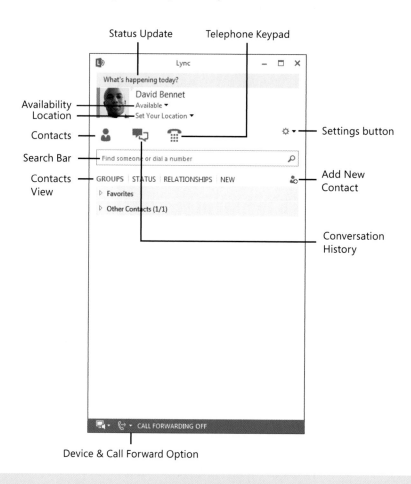

Tabbed conversations

A major component of any unified communications platform is instant messaging, and as you would expect, Lync 2013 has improved the experience still further by making it easier for you to manage your instant message environment.

To improve the overall user experience and your ability as a user to manage and navigate between the multiple instant messaging sessions you have open, Lync has introduced tabbed conversations.

Historically, each instant message session or conversation required its own separate window, which could be quite tricky to manage and switch between as the number of individual conversations increased. With tabbed conversations, Lync provides you with a single window with which to manage all instant message sessions, simplifying the way you navigate between each conversation and removing the need to have multiple instant message windows open on the taskbar.

Create a tabbed conversation

1 In the Search box, begin typing the name of the contact with whom you want to initiate a new instant message conversation.

2 On the Quick Lync Bar, click the Instant Message icon.

(continued on next page)

Create a tabbed conversation *(continued)*

3 The new conversation is placed in the tabbed conversation window, above any existing conversations.

3 ——

The Video Capable notification

Another new feature introduced in Lync 2013 is the addition of the Video Capable notification to the contact card. This informs you whether individual contacts are webcam-enabled, and thus capable of adding video to the call. In the accompanying illustration, the contact card for this individual clearly displays that this contact can accept video.

The Presenting presence status

The delivery of presence provides your contacts with real-time information as to your current availability, and in so doing, provides them with an expectation as to the likelihood of you responding.

Often, even when you set your presence to Busy, an individual will send you an instant message to gauge your ability to answer the call, or even just to ask a quick question.

In most situations, this is good practice because both parties can communicate without being completely distracted from what they were doing. After all, your status was set to Busy for a reason.

However, in certain situations the receipt of an instant message can be both inconvenient, and a little off-putting. For example, imagine that you are providing a demonstration to a class, and throughout the session you receive a number of instant messages. If you're the only one viewing the screen, this isn't too much of a problem, but it's not acceptable if your laptop is connected to a projector.

To prevent that from happening, Lync 2013 now offers the Presenting presence option. You can't select this option manually; it displays automatically as soon as you connect a projector to your laptop or share your desktop.

Multiparty HD video conferencing

Video conferencing is one of the areas that were the beneficiary of a major overhaul in Lync 2013. Video conferencing has always been a great feature of Lync, because it provides an easy to navigate and manage environment that many other systems couldn't match, while also providing a level of quality voice and video rarely experienced outside of the expensive dedicated audio and visual conference suites at larger organizations.

Within Lync, Microsoft has added the ability to view multiple participants within your online meeting. Historically, only the current speaker was displayed, but with the addition of the Gallery view, either the last five speakers or a preselected group of attendees can be viewed in the same window as the current speaker, enhancing the overall experience for all participants in the call. Joining an online meeting and experiencing the new Gallery view is straightforward.

Join an online meeting

1 Start Outlook and select Calendar.

2 On the calendar, double-click the meeting invitation.

(continued on next page)

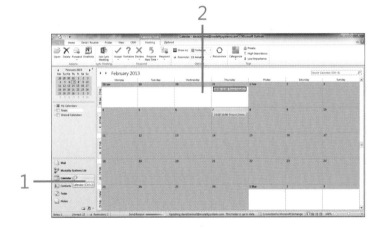

Join an online meeting (continued)

3 Click Join Online Meeting.

4 The Gallery view appears as attendees join the meeting.

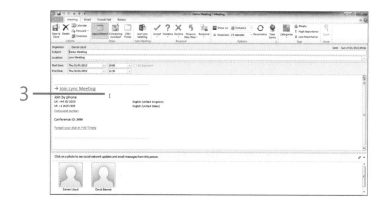

Introducing persistent chat (group chat)

Persistent chat is a new feature provided within the Lync 2013 client. With persistent chat, you can set up dedicated topic-based chat rooms that can improve communication and collaboration between geographically or departmentally dispersed teams.

Persistent chat rooms are predominantly set up for specific projects or areas of work so that members of the project teams can discuss elements of work, or provide updates in relation to progress.

Chat rooms are essentially dedicated workspaces in which members can post questions or responses to questions via instant messages. Messages contained within the room remain for a configurable amount of time, and each chat room can be moderated to ensure its appropriate use.

Creating a new chat room

Lync 2013 provides you with the ability to create new persistent chat rooms for the projects you are leading or for topics in which you share an interest with other members of your organization. For instance, you might be leading a project to improve productivity within the workplace, and you want a common venue where people can input their thoughts and suggestions or simply provide an update to team members. Alternatively, you might just have an interest in a particular sporting activity and want to set up a chat room for likeminded colleagues and coworkers to share experiences or post details of upcoming events. The point is, persistent chat rooms are designed to speed up access to knowledge and information, and, in the process, encourage awareness and participation.

Create a new chat room

1 Click the Persistent Chat icon.

2 Click the Add icon.

3 On the menu that appears, click Create A Chat Room.

4 On the Manage Persistent Chat Rooms page, click in the Domain\ User Name and Password text boxes and enter your credentials.

5 Click Sign In.

(continued on next page)

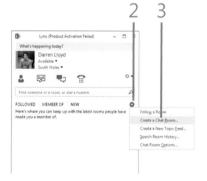

> **TIP** After you've selected the Persistent Chat icon, as an alternative to clicking the Add icon, you can also press Ctrl+R on your keyboard to create a new chat room.

Create a new chat room *(continued)*

6 On the My Rooms page, click Create A New Room.

7 On the Create A Room page, in the Room Name section, enter the name of the new chat room.

8 Provide a description of the room.

9 In the Privacy section, select the privacy level.

10 In the Members section, insert the first and last names of colleagues and coworkers to whom who you want to grant membership in your new chat room. Click the User Lookup icon to confirm and then click Create.

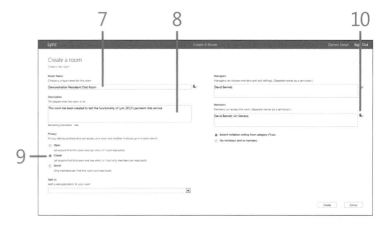

Following a chat room

Depending on the security levels of individual persistent chat rooms in Lync 2013, you might be able to add it to the list of rooms that you follow. Following persistent chat rooms doesn't grant you permission to post comments to it, but you can view updates posted by its members. This is particularly useful when you are not directly involved with the primary focus of the chat room, but you have a secondary interest in its content, perhaps because it impacts in some way on your own work (or interest).

Follow a chat room

1 Click the Persistent Chat icon and then, in the Search box, type the name of the room that you want to follow.

2 Hover the mouse pointer over the room and then, on the Quick Lync Bar, click the Add icon.

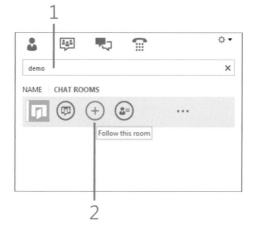

TIP   After your search for a persistent chat room has returned its result, you can right-click the desired result and then, on the shortcut menu that appears, click Add to follow the room.

Getting started with Lync 2013

3

To take advantage of the features that Microsoft Lync 2013 has to offer, the first task you must complete is that of signing in. When you sign in, you open a window to a fundamentally different way of communicating and collaborating with your contacts. With this single Lync client, you can view your contacts availability, converse with them via instant message (IM), send and receive email, make voice and video calls, and set up conferences (audio, video, and web), all right there at your fingertips.

Using Lync is simple and easily accomplished due to the intuitive design and layout of the Lync 2013 client. The ability to provide your contacts with as much detail about your availability, location, and preferred method of communication via notes and status updates will become second nature, and in doing so, you will improve the overall communications experience for all.

Over the following pages I'll guide you through the Lync 2013 sign-in process and provide an in-depth overview of the Lync 2013 client and its features.

In this section:

- Signing in to Lync 2013
- Changing your sign-in credentials
- Using the presence status
- Viewing integrated presence
- Understanding the presence status indicators
- Changing your status manually
- Making use of location status
- Adding a note to your status
- Using the Contact view options
- Maintaining conversation history
- Using the phone

Signing in to Lync 2013

So, you're eager to take advantage of the improved levels of communication and collaboration that you've been told Lync 2013 provides, and you're looking forward to being able to see the real-time availability of your colleagues and coworkers that

will prevent you from wasting your time calling them when they're unavailable. Well, to access this great functionality, along with the other tools that will fundamentally change the way you work, first you must sign in.

Start Lync 2013

1 On Windows 8 Start screen, double-click the Lync 2013 tile.

Sign in to Lync 2013

1 On the Sign In page of the Lync client window, click the Sign-In Address box and enter your user name.

2 In the Password text box, enter your password.

3 If you want Lync to remember your password, select the Save My Password check box.

(continued on next page)

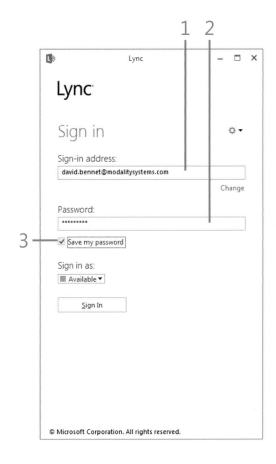

Sign in to Lync 2013 *(continued)*

4 If you selected the Save My password check box, in the pop-up message box that asks you to confirm that you want Lync to save your sign-in credentials, click Yes.

Changing your sign-in credentials

You might not always want to sign in to Lync 2013 with the exact same credentials. For example, perhaps you have a training account set up to demonstrate Lync 2013 to colleagues and new members joining your team, or you might have a separate account configured for testing purposes. Either way, you're going to need to sign in as someone else, and to do so, you need to be able to change your standard sign-in credentials.

Change your sign-in credentials

1   In the Lync client window, click the Settings icon (the small gear graphic). On the menu that appears, point to Tools and then, on the submenu that opens, click Options.

(continued on next page)

Change your sign-in credentials (continued)

2 In the Lync Options dialog box, click the Personal tab.

3 In the My Account section, in the Sign-In Address text box, enter the credentials that you want to use and then click OK. The next time you sign out you'll be asked to sign in with the new credentials.

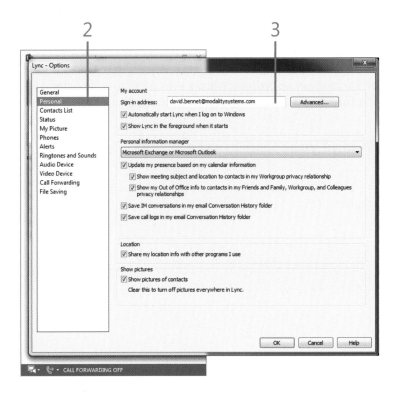

TIP From this point forward, each time you sign in to Lync, you will do so using the new credentials you entered in step 3 of this task. To revert to your original sign-in credentials, repeat steps 1 through 3.

Using the presence status

Of all the features incorporated into Lync 2013, presence is the "killer app" that will contribute more to your productivity than any other. Presence shows the real-time availability of your contacts, and in so doing, dramatically reduces the time you spend "blind-calling" colleagues and coworkers, only to get no answer, or find that you've been forwarded to a voicemail service.

Presence will have an immediate positive impact on your daily productivity. Just being able to see the availability of a contact lets you know whether she is available to help you with a question, or whether you should direct your query to other colleagues.

Viewing integrated presence

Presence is integrated into many other applications within
the Microsoft product portfolio, meaning if you have a query
relating to an email you've been sent, or a document stored
within SharePoint that you are collaborating on, you can see
the availability of the author from within the application and
then select the preferred method by which to communicate
with them. There is no need to switch to the Lync 2013 client
to initiate the conversation.

View-integrated presence in Microsoft SharePoint

You can view the contact card and availability of a document's author by hovering over the name of the author from
within SharePoint.

Understanding the presence status indicators

Lync 2013 provides a number of predetermined presence options that you can select manually, or that are updated automatically based on information obtained from within your Microsoft Outlook Calendar. It can also be set based on a period of non-activity. Presence is used to provide your contacts with a real-time understanding of your availability so that they can make an informed decision as to when and how best to contact you.

Use presence options

Lync 2013 provides the following options from which you can choose when setting your presence.

- Available
- Busy
- Do Not Disturb
- Be Right Back
- Off Work
- Appear Away
- Appear Offline

Options to Sign Out and Exit are also provided.

Changing your status manually

Lync 2013 makes it easy for you to manually change your presence and inform your coworkers of your availability. With just a couple of clicks, you can let your colleagues know when it's a good time (or not) to contact you.

Change your status

1 In the Lync client window, click your current presence status.

2 In the list that appears, choose the presence status that you want to be displayed to your co-workers.

The presence indicator now displays your changed status.

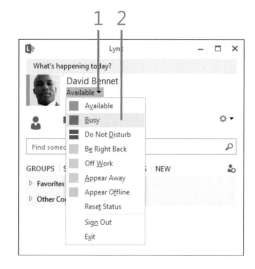

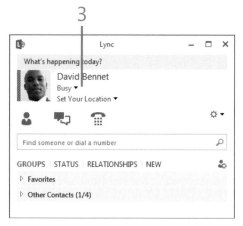

Making use of location status

Using Lync 2013, you can sign in using numerous devices and from any location (providing that you have access to the Internet). As a result, it's helpful for your colleagues and coworkers to know where exactly you're currently working. Your presence might be set to Available, but that doesn't mean you're working from your office on the next floor up. To save your coworkers from a wasted trip when you might not even on the same continent, set your location as well as your availability.

Set your location

1 In the Lync client window, click the Location drop-down arrow.

2 In the list that appears, either select one of the locations displayed or type a new location in the box, and then press Enter.

> ✓ **TIP** To stop displaying your location, click the Location box and then, on the list that appears, clear the Show Others My Location check box.

> ✓ **TIP** Each time you sign in to Lync 2013 from a new location, enter the location. The next time you sign in from that location, Lync 2013 will remember it and display that location.

Adding a note to your status

In addition to displaying your location, Lync 2013 also provides you with the ability to add a note to your current status. The note will appear on your contact card when viewed by others. This is a great way to provide an additional piece of information about what you are currently engaged with, or indeed, your preferred method of communication. For example, you might be working on an important task and only want to be contacted if it's urgent, and only via instant messages. Alternatively, you might be travelling and want to leave another number at which others can contact you.

Add a note

1 At the top of the Lync client window, click in the Note text box.

2 Type the message that you want others to see and then press Return.

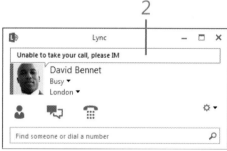

 TIP The notes field is also automatically populated with the Out Of Office reply you create in Microsoft Outlook.

 TIP To remove your note repeat step 1, delete the existing entry and then press Enter.

Using the Contact view options

Lync 2013 provides a number of methods by which you can display your contacts, making it easier and more efficient to find those with whom you want to communicate. As your list of contacts increase, you'll find it easier to search and find them if you've stored them in a group relevant to their role, department, company, or relationship to you.

You learn how to create new groups in Section 4, "Managing contacts," but in the meantime, I'll show you how to locate contacts based on the default views provided in Lync 2013: Status, Relationship, and also New people who have recently added you to their contacts list.

Change Contact view

1 In the Lync client window, with the Groups tab selected, click the Contacts button.

2 To view by availability, click the Status tab.

(continued on next page)

✓ **TIP**   You can also change the way in which your contacts are displayed by clicking the Add Contact button, located to the right of the tabs, and choosing Display Options. You can select whether to display pictures as well as the order in which contacts are presented.

Change Contact view (continued)

3 To view by a contact's relationship to you, click the Relationships tab.

4 To view individuals who have added you to their contact list, click the New tab.

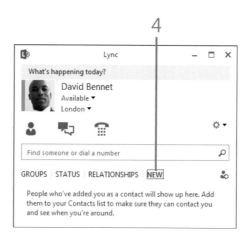

Maintaining conversation history

Lync 2013 provides a number of ways in which to communicate and collaborate with your colleagues and coworkers, and it's sometimes important to have a record of calls and conversations that have taken place.

More often than not, the instant messages you send and receive will contain information relating to tasks that you need to complete, so the ability to review past correspondence is an important function of any unified communications platform.

Lync provides a dedicated area in which to view past instant messages and telephone calls. In addition, it provides a number of categorized views in which to display them, including All conversations, Missed conversations, and a category for calls and conference calls.

View your conversation history

1 In the Lync client window, click the Conversations button.

2 By default, the All tab is displayed.

(continued on next page)

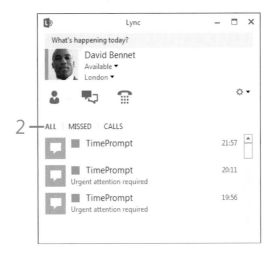

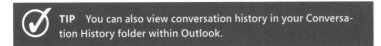

TIP   You can also view conversation history in your Conversation History folder within Outlook.

View your conversation history *(continued)*

3 To view missed telephone calls and instant messages, click the Missed tab.

4 To view telephone calls and conference calls, click the Calls tab.

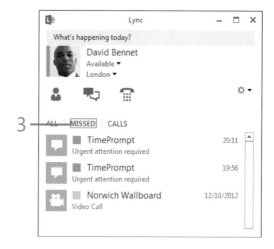

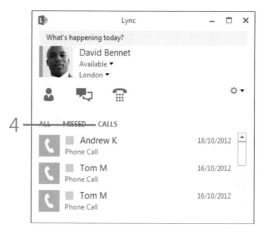

Using the phone

Lync 2013 comes equipped with a phone keypad that you can use to call individuals who are not already in your contact list. The phone also provides you with the ability to listen to the voicemails you've received as well as setting and changing your voicemail greeting.

In addition, the phone has a great feature with which you can check the quality of your calls by making a test call, which is

ideal when you're connected via Wi-Fi on an unfamiliar network. It also provides the option to set your PIN for dial-in into conferences.

Guidance on using and setting up your personal telephony environment is discussed in more detail in Section 8, "Using the Lync 2013 voice features," through Section 11, "Reviewing your voicemail from within Outlook."

Dial a number

1 In the Lync client window, click the Phone button.

(continued on next page)

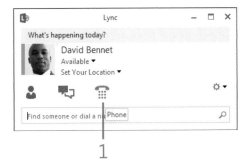

TIP You can also make a call by inserting an individual's telephone number into the Search box and pressing enter.

Dial a number *(continued)*

2 On the keypad that appears, click each number of the telephone number of the person whom you want to contact.

3 Click Call.

> ![check] **TIP** If Lync 2013 recognizes the number you enter as belonging to that of a contact whom you have stored in Lync or Outlook, it will return the name of the individual instead of the dialed number in the Name box.

Managing contacts

4

Let's face it, your contacts are important to you, so the ability to search, add, and categorize them is a fundamental requirement of any communication platform.

Searching for contacts in Microsoft Lync 2013 is straightforward, and the information returned on each contact can be extremely comprehensive. Gone are the days when you need to reference a book or intranet page to find a colleague's telephone number. And similarly, gone are the days when you need to type a contact's telephone number to call her; just type her name in the search box and you'll be provided with a host of information related to her availability, alternative contact numbers, location, and even information relating to her ability to join a video call.

Lync 2013 has made finding your contacts as simple as it can be, and after you have located them, it provides you with a host of methods by which to communicate.

In this section, I'll guide you through the process of searching for your contacts, adding them to a group you've just created, and even tagging a contact so that you're alerted the very second she becomes available.

In this section:

- Searching contacts
- Creating a new contact group
- Adding contacts to a group
- Adding external contacts to a group
- Removing a contact from a group
- Monitoring a contact's availability

Searching contacts

Searching for contacts in Lync 2013 is simple, and the information returned will assist you greatly in understanding their availability as well as the best method by which to initiate a conversation with them. For instance, the accompanying screenshot shows that Jim is "Inactive," and also that he has signed into Lync 2013 by using his mobile. You can try sending an instant message, but actually your best chance of reaching Jim is probably going to be via a call to his mobile.

When searching for contacts, Lync 2013 looks at the contacts you have stored in Microsoft Outlook in addition to those you have available in Lync.

Search for a contact

1 In the Lync client window, click in the search box.

2 Type the name of the individual whom you wish to contact.

3 Lync returns the contact card for that individual. (Note the additional information stating that Jim is signed into Lync 2013 with his mobile.)

(continued on next page)

Search for a contact *(continued)*

4 Hover over the contact card to display the Quick Lync bar, which presents communications options (instant message, telephone, or video).

✓ **TIP** To view additional ways of communicating with and managing your contacts, on the contact card, click the More Options button (the ellipsis to the right of the other options).

✓ **TIP** If you are using a touch-enabled device, you can't hover over items as you can with a mouse pointer. So, to display the Quick Lync bar as instructed in step 4, tap the picture of the contact with whom you want to communicate.

Creating a new contact group

Lync 2013 provides a number of predefined groups in which to save your contacts, but what if you want to create your own groups? You can create groups in Lync 2013 with ease and save your contacts in a more meaningful manner, and in a way, that helps you to locate them more easily.

Create a new group

1 In the Lync client window, with the Groups tab selected, click the Add a Contact icon.

(continued on next page)

✓ **TIP** You can also create a new group by pressing Ctrl+N.

Create a new group *(continued)*

2 On the menu that appears, click the Create A New Group command.

3 Below the existing groups, in the text box that appears, type the name of your new group and then press Return.

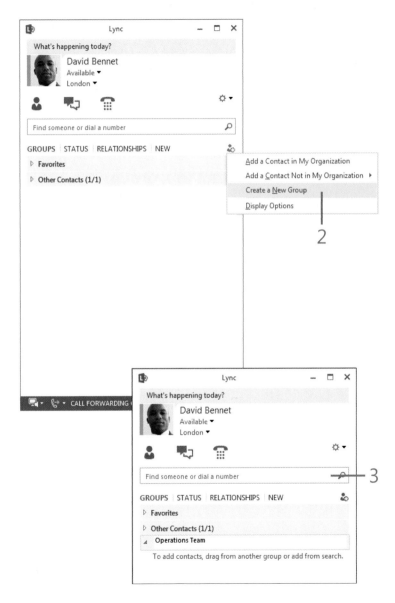

Adding contacts to a group

After you've completed your search for a contact, wouldn't it be great to add them to a group so that you could find them more quickly the next time?

By default, Lync 2013 provides you with three predefined groups in which to store your contacts. These groups are

Favorites, Other Contacts, and Frequent Contacts, which as the name suggests is a list of contacts that you correspond with most frequently. You can also create your own groups as described in "Create a new group" on page 40.

You can add both internal and external contacts to your groups.

Add an internal contact to a group

1 In the Lync client window, click the search box and type the name of a colleague.

2 Hover over the contact card to display the Quick Lync bar and then click the More Options button (the ellipsis to the right of the other options).

(continued on next page)

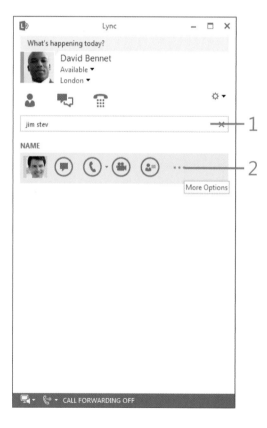

TIP You can also press Ctrl+O to add an individual to a contact list.

Add an internal contact to a group *(continued)*

3 On the menu that appears, point to Add To Contacts List.

4 On the submenu that appears, click the group in which you want to save the contact.

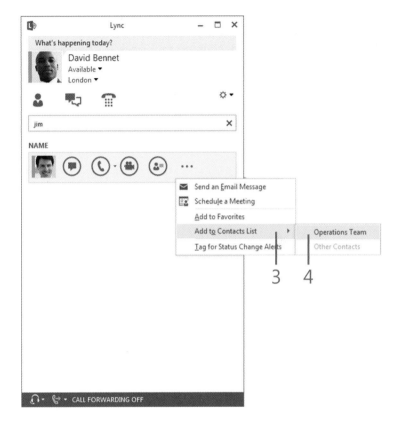

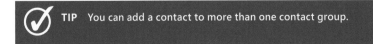

TIP You can add a contact to more than one contact group.

Adding external contacts to a group

Just as you can add internal contacts to your Lync 2013 groups, you can also add contacts from outside your company or organization.

Add an external contact

1 In the Lync client window, in the search box, type the email address of the external contact.

2 Hover over the contact card to display the Quick Lync bar and then click the More Options ellipsis (the ellipsis to the right of the other options).

3 On the menu that appears, point to Add To Contact List.

4 On the submenu that appears, click the contact list to which you want to add your contact.

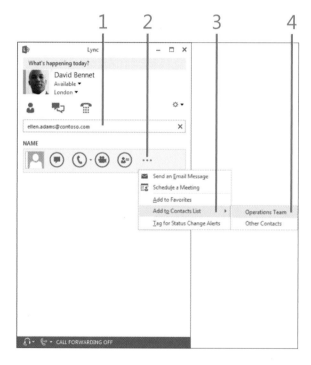

✓ **TIP** Presence information for external contacts will only be provided if they too are using Lync 2013 (or previous versions) and their company allows them to share presence information. Presence will also be shown if the external contact is signed into a supported Public IM service; for example, a Microsoft Account.

Removing a contact from a group

Managing your contacts is important to maintaining an up-to-date address book, and from time to time, the need might arise for you to remove a contact from a Lync 2013 group, or indeed, remove it permanently from your address book. Removing contacts helps to keep your address book tidy and free from unnecessary contact details that you no longer use or require. It also means your search results will be returned quicker and the need to scroll through a long list of possible contacts when entering a partial name will be reduced.

Remove a contact from a group

1 In the Lync client window, view the group to which the contact belongs.

(continued on next page)

Remove a contact from a group *(continued)*

2 Right-click the contact card and then, on the shortcut menu that appears, click Remove From Group.

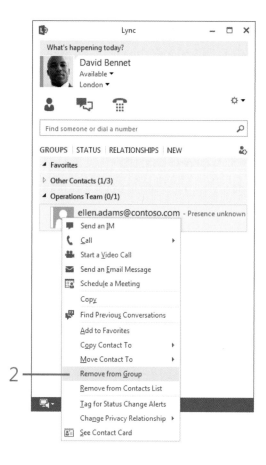

2

Monitoring a contact's availability

Have you ever endured the experience in which you need to speak to a colleague or coworker urgently, only to find he's not available, and then spend the rest of the day calling and leaving him voice messages in the hope that he'll respond? Me too!

I previously discussed how presence provides you with information relating to a contact's availability, so the chances are, if you see he is not available, you're not going to call him. You could instead look to someone else to assist you; however, if it's only

that specific contact with whom you need to communicate, calling someone else isn't a viable option, either.

A really useful tool provided within Lync 2013 is the ability to monitor the availability of a contact and then receive notification when his status changes. Commonly referred to as *tagging*, this feature is used to inform you of any change in a contact's presence, meaning you'll be alerted as soon as he becomes available.

Tag a contact for status change alerts

1 Using the search function, locate the contact with whom you want to communicate.

2 Hover over the contact card to display the Quick Lync bar and then click the More Options button (the ellipsis to the right of the other options).

3 On the menu that appears, choose the Tag For Status Change Alerts command.

(continued on next page)

TIP If you are using a touch-enabled device, you can't hover over items as you can with a mouse pointer. So, to display the Quick Lync bar as instructed in step 2, tap the picture of the contact with whom you want to communicate.

Tag a contact for status change alerts (continued)

4 In the pop-up message box that informs you that tagged contacts will be added to your contacts list, click OK.

5 When the individual's status changes, you'll be alerted via an instant message.

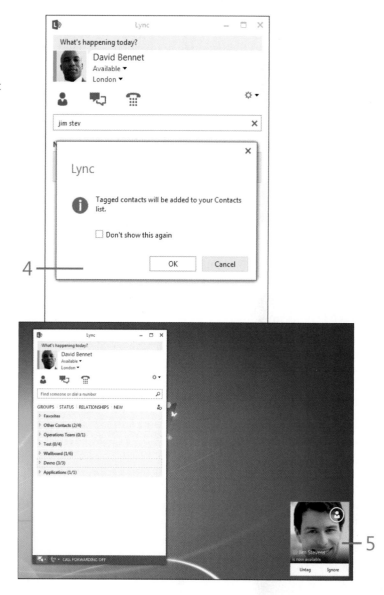

Starting a conversation

5

One of the first tasks you will likely want to accomplish after you've signed in to Microsoft Lync 2013 is to locate a colleague or coworker and start a conversation.

Lync 2013 provides a number of modalities from which to initiate a conversation as well as a host of other pointers that are designed to give you a good idea of which modality to use in any given situation. Section 3, "Getting started with Lync 2013," discusses presence, location, and notes. By using the information these provide, you will have good idea of how best to communicate with individual colleagues and coworkers.

In this section, we focus on initiating a conversation by using an instant message (IM). IMs are a quick and easy way by which to ask and receive responses to questions and advance your work much more efficiently. I frequently choose IMs as my preferred method by which to communicate when I need to ask simple or basic questions that do not require a prolonged response. Additionally, I also use IMs in the first instance when I can see that the status of a colleague or coworker is "Busy," but I want to know if they are free to join a quick telephone call or have an opportunity to answer a quick question via IM.

In this section:

- Sending an IM
- Marking a conversation as "high importance"
- Changing the font of your IM
- Hiding the IM area
- Inviting additional contacts to a conversation
- Creating tabbed conversations
- Popping a tabbed conversation to a separate window
- Closing tabbed conversations
- Sending and receiving files within an IM
- Escalating an IM to a voice or video call

Sending an IM

From experience, I can truthfully state that IMs will be the most-used modality from within your Lync 2013 unified communications (UC) toolkit. Sending an IM is as simple as one-two-three. And, the fact that they elicit an almost instant response means that they are the tool of choice when you need a quick and brief answer to a question.

IMs save you time. When you need a quick response to move a task forward, IMs are the tool for you. If you were to send an email, you might have to wait until the recipient next opens his inbox before receiving a reply. Additionally, you might call a colleague or coworker and not receive a response. By their very nature, IMs imply that you need a quick response, and they provide the recipient with the ability to oblige you immediately, with very little effort, providing you with the details you require with the least amount of disruption.

Send an IM

1 In the Lync client window, click the search box and enter the name of the person to whom you want to send an instant message.

2 Hover over that person's contact card to display the Quick Lync bar and then click the Instant Message button.

(continued on next page)

1

2

✓ **TIP** If you are using a touch-enabled device, you can't hover over items as you can with a mouse pointer. So, to display the Quick Lync bar as instructed in step 2, tap the picture of the contact with whom you want to communicate.

Send an IM *(continued)*

3 In the conversation window, type your message and wait for a response.

4 The recipient's response will appear in the conversation window.

Marking a conversation as "high importance"

We've already discussed how IM recipients have a tendency to respond fairly quickly. Indeed, they typically respond much quicker than if they were responding to an email. However, on occasions you might want to give a further indication of the importance of a specific IM.

Just as with emails, you can mark an IM as being of high importance, providing its recipient with an indication of the urgency to which you require a response.

Mark a conversation as high importance

1 In the Lync client window, click the search box and enter the name of the person to whom you want to send an instant message.

2 Hover over that person's contact card to display the Quick Lync bar and then click the Instant Message button.

(continued on next page)

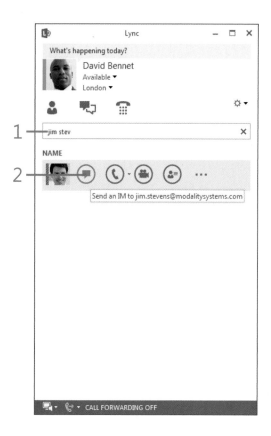

Mark a conversation as high importance *(continued)*

3 In the conversation window, click the Set High Importance For This Message button.

4 In the conversation area, type your message, press Enter, and then wait for a response.

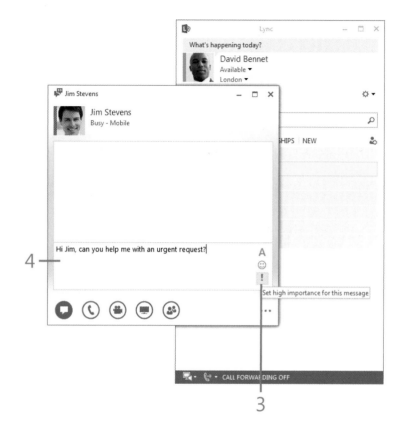

Changing the font of your IM

IMs are a fantastic way to communicate, and you can even do a little customization to add a personal touch to the messages you send. Changing the font of your IMs is easily achieved within Lync 2013. There is a wide range of fonts, sizes, and colors from which you can choose, together with other familiar formatting options such as bold and italics.

Change your IM font

1 From within the existing IM conversation window, click the Font button.

(continued on next page)

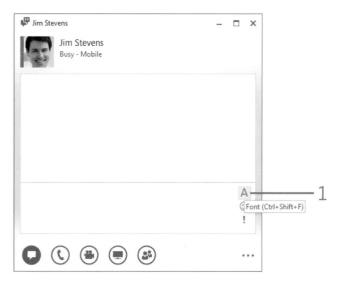

Change your IM font *(continued)*

2 From the menu that appears, choose the font that you want to apply.

3 Click the conversation window and begin typing your instant message.

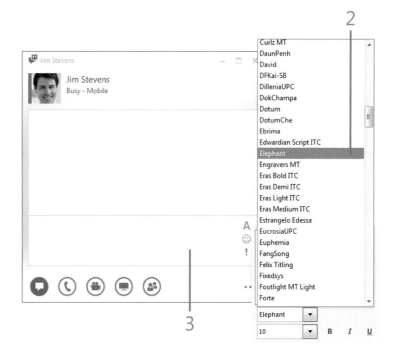

TIP You can also change the color and size of the font on the same menu.

Hiding the IM area

When you're participating in a call or conference, it's possible hide the IM conversation window so that you can focus on the call itself or, indeed, the content that is being shared within the Lync 2013 extendable window.

Hide the IM area

1 From within the existing conversation window, click the Instant Message button.

2 The IM area is now hidden.

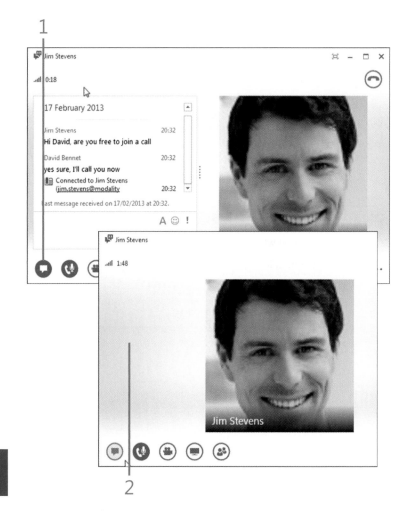

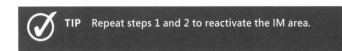
TIP Repeat steps 1 and 2 to reactivate the IM area.

Inviting additional contacts to a conversation

As we've already demonstrated, initiating an IM conversation within Lync 2013 is a pretty simple process: just select the individual with whom you want to have a conversation, click the IM button, and then type your message.

However, the answers we require might not be that easy to come by, and it sometimes needs the input of additional parties to find what you're looking for or to make a decision.

For instance, a customer requires a particular product from your catalog and requires it to be delivered on a certain date. Using IM, it's easy to initiate a conversation with a colleague from the particular department to ensure that the product is in stock, but how can you confirm that it can be dispatched in time to meet

the customer's requirements? You're going to need to confirm with a colleague in shipping for that, so wouldn't it be great to add that individual to your existing conversation so that he can see the previous comments. After all, he might have a delivery scheduled to the same area where your customer resides and on the specific day, but how big is the product, and is there room?

It's easy to turn what was a standard IM session into a conference between multiple parties, and as demonstrated in the preceding scenario, you can gain all the information required via IM, all while the customer is still on the phone, enhancing her experience and saving you time in the process!

Invite additional contacts

1 Find the individual whom you want to add to the conversation.

2 Drag the individual into the existing IM conversation.

(continued on next page)

Invite additional contacts *(continued)*

3 You've now turned a standard IM conversation into a conference.

3

Creating tabbed conversations

As we've already pointed out, using IM is a great way to get quick answers to questions, and therefore it's a modality that is adopted very quickly across organizations. As a result, not only will you be sending IMs, but so will your colleagues and coworkers. This means you can have multiple IM session windows open on your desktop, and as they increase, you might find it increasingly difficult to manage them all.

To improve the overall user experience as well as your ability to manage and navigate between multiple sessions, Lync 2013 has introduced tabbed conversations.

Prior to this release of Lync 2013, each instant message session or conversation required its own separate window, which could be quite fiddly to manage and switch between as the number of separate conversations increased. With tabbed conversations, Lync 2013 provides a single window in which to manage all IM sessions, simplifying the way you navigate between each conversation and removing the need to have multiple IM windows open on the taskbar.

Create tabbed conversations

1 Open an IM conversation with a contact.

(continued on next page)

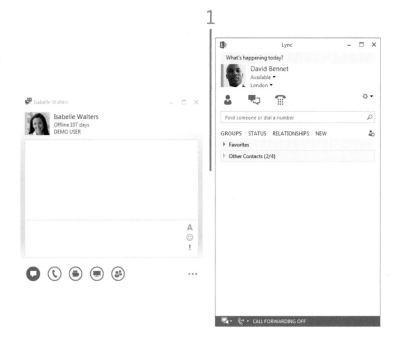

Create tabbed conversations (continued)

2 Click the main Lync client window. In the Search box, type the name of another contact with whom you want to communicate.

3 Hover over that person's contact card to display the Quick Lync bar and then click the Instant Message icon.

4 Both conversations now appear in a tabbed conversation window.

Popping a tabbed conversation to a separate window

There might be an occasion when you feel the need to remove a particular IM conversation from within the tabbed conversation window, viewing it instead within a separate window.

Pop a tabbed conversation to a separate window

1 Select the conversation that you want to open in a separate IM window.

2 In the upper-right corner of the conversation window, click the Pop This Conversation Out button.

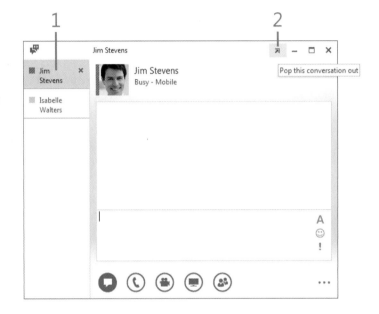

✓ **TIP** To return a popped conversation to the tabbed conversation window, select the conversation that you want to return and then, in the upper-right corner, select the Pop This Conversation In button.

Closing tabbed conversations

After you've finished a particular IM session, it's good practice to close it down. Not only will this make room for new sessions, but it also makes it easier to navigate the tabbed conversation window.

Close a tabbed conversation

1 In the tabbed conversation window, click the tab of the session that you want to close and then, in the upper-right corner of the window, click the Close button.

2 In the pop-up message box that appears, click either Close Current Tab or Close All Tabs.

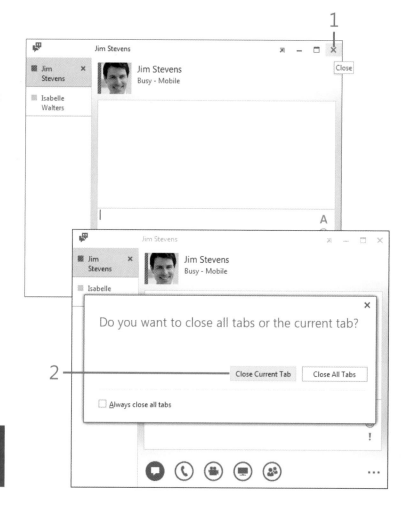

> **TIP** You can also close individual sessions by clicking the Close buttons (x) on each conversation, which are located in the left pane of the tabbed conversation window.

Sending and receiving files within an IM

During communication, there is often a need to discuss a specific element of work or request additional supporting information. More often than not, this results in a colleague or coworker sending you an email with attachments containing the information you need. Lync 2013 simplifies this process by making it possible for you to send and receive documents from within an IM session.

Send a file

1 From within an existing conversation window, hover over the Manage Presentable Content button.

(continued on next page)

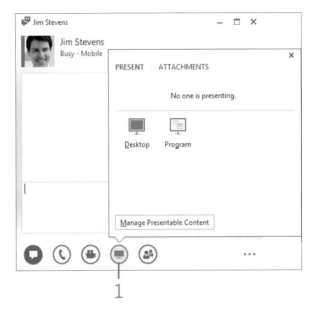

 TIP Your administrator might block specific file types or all file transfers completely.

Send a file *(continued)*

2 At the top of the dialog box that opens, click Attachments.

3 Click Add Attachment.

4 In the Send A File To All Participants dialog box, select the file that you want to send and then click Open.

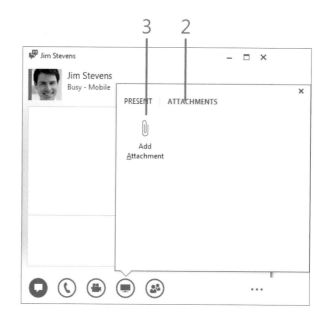

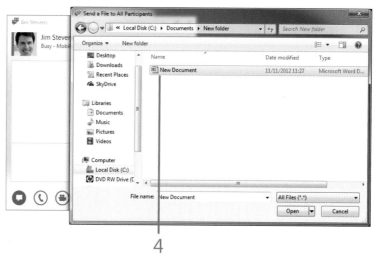

Receive a file

1 From within an existing conversation window, click the displayed file icon to receive it.

Escalating an IM to a voice or video call

On occasion, you might find that what started off as a very basic query via IM has turned into something more complex, and it would be easier to continue the conversation on the telephone.

The process of adding voice or even video (if your device is video-capable) to an existing IM session is extremely simple, and because it's achieved in the same window, you don't need to open a new session to make the call, thus keeping the number of active windows that you have open at any one time to a minimum.

Escalate an IM to a voice call

1 From within an active IM conversation window, hover over the Call button.

2 On the menu that appears, click the number that you want to call.

 TIP To escalate an IM session to a video call, in the active IM conversation window, hover over the Video button and then, on the menu that appears, click Start My Video.

 TIP You can also start a video call by pressing Ctrl+S when you're in an active IM session.

Collaborating with your contacts

6

Microsoft Lync 2013 has been designed to provide you with a suite of tools that aid communication and collaboration with your colleagues and coworkers. Lync provides you with the ability to work from any location, whether it's your office, your home, or at your favorite coffee shop. However, working from any location is one thing, but if you don't have the tools you need to work efficiently and effectively, you're not going to be productive.

Lync 2013 offers a multitude of ways to help you and your colleagues increase your productivity, but more important to you, they can help make your life easier.

Included within the Lync 2013 productivity suite of tools is the ability to set up ad hoc or preplanned conferences (audio, video, or web) and share your desktop, files, or programs; you can even create whiteboards, and PowerPoint presentations on which you and your colleagues can collaborate.

Over the next few pages I'll take you through each tool, step by step, so that by the end you'll be confident with them all and can start reaping the benefits of your new productive lifestyle.

Sending an email to a contact

Sending email to a contact might seem like a stone-age thing to do from a unified communications (UC) platform, especially when you consider the other communication modalities that are at your disposal. However, Lync 2013 does not discriminate, and email is actually still a really useful feature to have available.

Consider this: you need to speak with a colleague or coworker, you've searched for the person in Lync to see if she's available, but her presence status is informing you that she's offline. You could call and leave a voice message, but it's actually going to

be easier to send her an email with your questions rather than leave a long-winded message. Now, imagine if you had to minimize Lync 2013 to open Microsoft Outlook to send the email—a long-winded process in its own right, I'm sure you'll agree.

With Lync 2013, you have the option to send an email directly from the contact card of your colleagues and coworkers, saving you from having to open another application. It's all about making life easier.

Send an email

1 In the Lync client window, click the Search box and enter the name of the person to whom you want to send an email.

2 Hover over that person's contact card to display the Quick Lync bar and then click the More Options ellipsis.

(continued on next page)

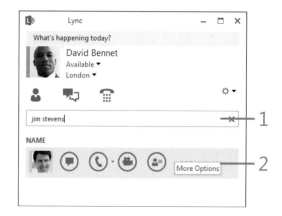

✓ **TIP**   If you are using a touch-enabled device, you can't hover over items as you can with a mouse pointer. So, to display the Quick Lync bar as instructed in step 2, tap the picture of the contact with whom you want to communicate.

Send an email (continued)

3 On the menu that appears, click the Send An Email Message command.

Scheduling a meeting

Scheduling meetings is another task that you probably complete on a regular basis. It can sometimes be the case that a face-to-face meeting is the best option in the first place, especially if you haven't met the individual before. In these situations, you could send an invite to an online conference call, which we will discuss later in the section, but you might consider a direct meeting to be more appropriate, and therefore you'll need to send an invite.

With this in mind, Lync 2013 again simplifies the process by providing you with the option to send a meeting invitation directly from an individual's contact card, reducing the number of steps required to complete the process.

Schedule a meeting

1 In the Lync client window, click the search box and enter the name of the person with whom you want to schedule a meeting.

2 Hover over that person's contact card to display the Quick Lync bar and then click the More Options ellipsis.

(continued on next page)

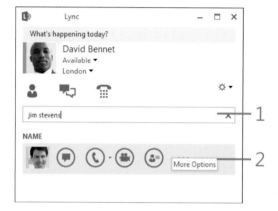

Schedule a meeting *(continued)*

3 On the menu that appears, click the Schedule A Meeting command.

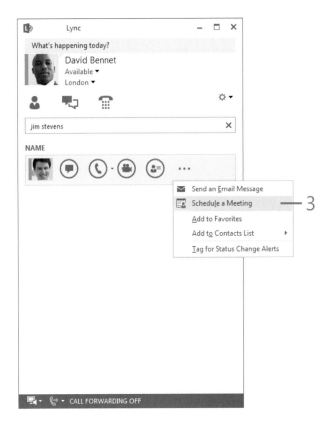

Sharing your desktop or program with others online

Imagine that you've managed to reach a colleague or contact, but you're finding it difficult to explain your query or the element of work with which you require assistance. It would be so much easier if you could share your desktop or the individual program you are using to provide your colleague with a real-time view of what you're trying to accomplish.

With Microsoft Lync 2013, you can do just that, and as you have probably come to expect, it's pretty simple.

Share your desktop or program

1 In the Lync client window, click the search box and enter the name of the person with whom you want to share your desktop.

2 Hover over that person's contact card to display the Quick Lync bar and then click the Instant Message button.

(continued on next page)

Share your desktop or program *(continued)*

3 At the bottom of the conversation window, click Manage Presentable Content.

4 At the upper-left of the dialog box that opens, click Present, if it is not already highlighted.

5 Select Desktop or Program, depending on what you want to share.

6 If you select Program, Lync 2013 will return a list of applications that are currently open on your computer. Click the program that you want to share.

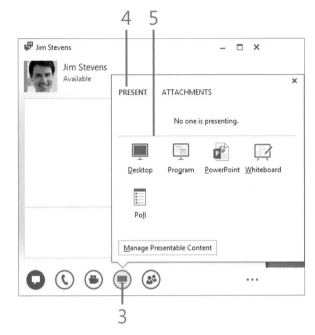

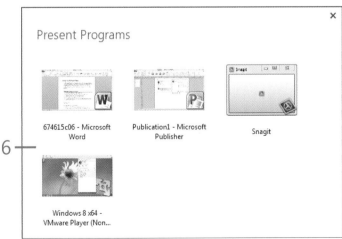

Sharing whiteboards or Microsoft PowerPoint presentations

In addition to sharing your desktop or program in Lync 2013, you can also choose to share a whiteboard, an existing Power-Point presentation, or even create a poll to gauge individual views and opinions on a particular subject. The ability to share these elements greatly enhances the collaboration experience that both you and your contacts can enjoy.

Share a whiteboard or PowerPoint presentation

1 In the Lync client window, click the Search box and enter the name of the person with whom you want to share a whiteboard or Power-Point presentation.

2 Hover over that person's contact card to display the Quick Lync bar and then click the Instant Message button.

(continued on next page)

Share a whiteboard or PowerPoint presentation *(continued)*

3 At the bottom of the conversation window, click Manage Presentable Content.

4 At the upper-left of the dialog box that opens, click Present, if it is not already highlighted.

5 Click either Whiteboard or PowerPoint, depending on what you want to share.

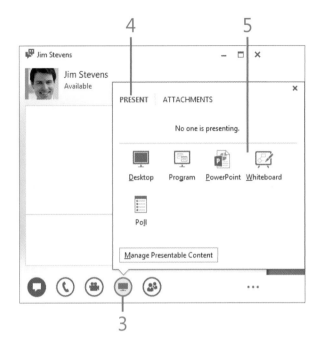

Creating online meetings

Lync 2013 is not just a *communication* platform; it's a *collaboration* platform with which you can team up with other individuals, both internal and external to your organization. There are many ways in which to do this, but the most common approach when collaborating with a number of individuals is to set up an online meeting. Online meetings can be audio, video, or web-based, and you can set them up at your convenience, either scheduled, or ad hoc.

Create an online meeting

1 Within Microsoft Outlook, on the ribbon, click the Home tab. In the New group, click New Items and then, on the menu, click Lync Meeting.

(continued on next page)

Create an online meeting (continued)

2 Enter the email address of the individuals you would like to attend the online meeting.

3 Click Send.

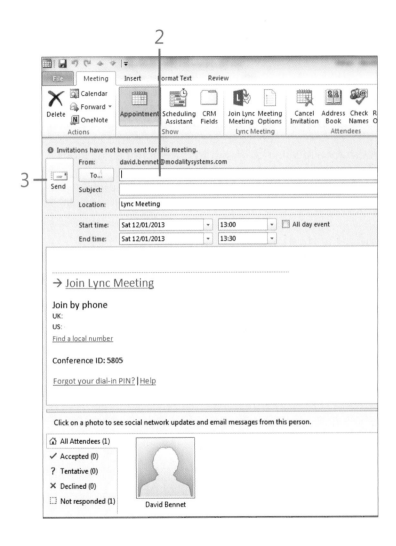

Joining online meetings

Online meetings provide the same functionality as standard person-to-person communications, such as sending instant messages, sharing your desktop or a program, or even creating a white board on which to jot down ideas. They are a great way to collaborate with colleagues and coworkers. Online meetings will also save you the hassle and time associated with booking a room for a meeting or having to travel to other locations.

Another area in which online meetings can be useful is when you're finding it difficult to align schedules. For example, you

need just 15 minutes of your manager's time, but there just doesn't seem to be a way to fit you in. Online meetings are great for quickly covering the set agenda and then moving on to your next appointment.

Finally, so you don't forget to join your online meeting, Outlook will send you a reminder a set period of time prior to the online meeting commencing. From within this notification you are able to join the meeting without having to open it within your Outlook Calendar.

Join an online meeting

1   In Outlook, click Calendar.

2   Double-click on the Online Meeting you wish to join.

(continued on next page)

Join an online meeting *(continued)*

3 Click the Join Lync Meeting link.

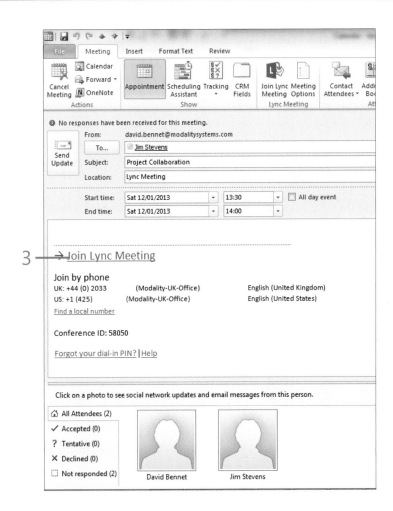

Online meeting reminders

Outlook will remind you of a scheduled meeting at a set period prior to its commencement by sending you a meeting reminder notification. You can join your online meeting by clicking the Join Online button, or you can choose to set a period of time before you are reminded again and click the Snooze button.

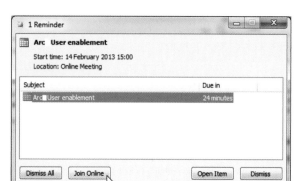

Using Lync with Microsoft Outlook

7

To help you become more productive within your working environment, Microsoft has designed Lync 2013 to integrate seamlessly with a number of key applications from within the company's core product portfolio. By lighting up the presence information of colleagues and coworkers from within these applications and providing you with the same functionality as if you were communicating directly from within the Lync 2013 client, Microsoft has removed the need to switch between applications, thus streamlining and simplifying your communication experience.

The key to this streamlined approach to communication is the integration of Lync 2013 with Microsoft Outlook. Over the next few pages, I will demonstrate how viewing the real-time presence of colleagues and coworkers from within Outlook not only saves you valuable work time, but also provides an intuitive and functional method by which you can respond to correspondence stored within your Outlook inbox.

In addition, this section also discusses the relevance and use of the Conversation History and Missed Call folders, setting your privacy relationships, and activating your Quick Contacts groups.

In this section:

- Viewing presence information within Outlook
- Integrating the Outlook calendar
- Responding to an email by using instant message
- Responding to an email via telephone
- Creating a Lync online meeting in Outlook
- Viewing the Conversation History folder
- Viewing the Missed Conversations folder
- Viewing the Missed Calls folder
- Viewing missed ad hoc conference calls
- Configuring your privacy settings
- Accessing online meetings via the Lync Web App

Viewing presence information within Outlook

As a result of the integration of Lync 2013 with Outlook, you can view the real-time presence of your Lync-enabled contacts. Each time you receive an email from a contact that is using Lync, you can see the contact's presence. The presence information displayed is actual real-time availability, not the availability at the time of sending the email. This provides you with a more accurate expectation as to their ability to respond to any queries that arose as part of the email you received.

Furthermore, if the email was sent to a number of recipients, the real-time presence of all recipients who use Microsoft Lync will be displayed.

Note in the accompanying screenshot how the presence information for the sender and recipients of an email is displayed.

The presence information is shown for both sender and recipient

Integrating the Outlook calendar

Calendar integration is an important part of the cross-functional relationship between Lync 2013 and Outlook because it automatically changes your real-time presence based on entries contained within your Outlook calendar. This integration makes it easier for your colleagues and coworkers to view your availability while simultaneously relieving you of the chore of manually changing your presence when you attend meetings or join conference calls.

With this level of integration, it's important that you utilize your Outlook calendar in a way that best reflects the activities you will be conducting, and also in a way that provides a true reflection of the duration you are likely to be engaged in those activities. The more detailed and relevant this information is, the more relevant your availability becomes when your presence is viewed by others.

Depending on the Privacy Relationship settings you have configured, people trying to contact you will either see that you are busy or will be provided with a more meaningful description of your availability; for example, "In a meeting" or "In a conference call."

In addition to providing information relating to your current availability, Lync 2013 also interrogates your Outlook calendar and displays information regarding how long you are available for a given day before you have a scheduled meeting, or if you are in a meeting, the time when you are scheduled to become available.

The accompanying screenshots show an example of an online meeting entry within an Outlook calendar and the corresponding "In a Conference Call" presence notification in Lync.

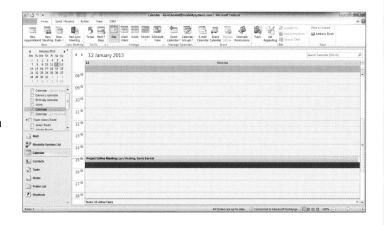

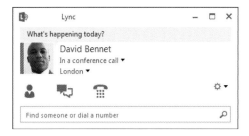

Responding to an email by using instant message

In addition to providing Lync 2013 presence information, users are also able to utilize the standard Lync modalities from within Outlook. This means that you do not need to leave the Outlook window to send instant messages (IMs), share and collaborate, or initiate audio and video calls. In fact, you're still using the Lync application, but you're able to access these features from within Outlook, which ultimately saves you time switching between applications on the desktop.

Respond to an email by using an IM

1 In Outlook, select the email to which you want to respond by IM.

2 Hover over the sender's name to display the contact card for that person.

3 On the contact card, click the Instant Message button and then, in the conversation window, type your message. Press Return to send the message.

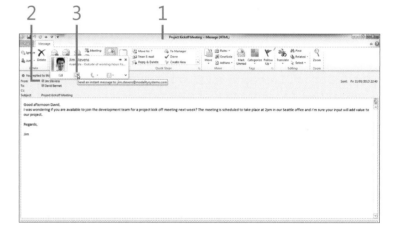

TIP When you respond to an email by using IM, the subject of the email appears at the top of the IM window, providing the recipient with an indication of the purpose of the communication.

TIP If you are using a touch-enabled device, you can't hover over items as you can with a mouse pointer. So, to display the contact card as instructed in step 2, tap the picture of the contact with whom you want to communicate.

Responding to an email via telephone

In some instances, you might feel that instead of responding to an email with another email or indeed an instant message, a telephone conversation would be more appropriate. In Outlook, it's easy to respond to an email by telephone.

Respond to an email by telephone

1 In Outlook, select the email to which you want to respond by phone.

2 Hover over the sender's name to display the contact card for that person.

3 On the contact card, click the Call button and then, on the menu that appears, click the number that you want to use.

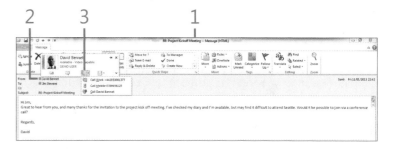

Creating a Lync online meeting in Outlook

Creating an online meeting is a fantastic way to bring your colleagues and coworkers together. Online meeting requests are created from within Microsoft Outlook and sent to attendees in the same way as traditional meeting invites, the only difference being that the meeting takes place online. Online meetings can be audio, video, and web-based, and you can set them up at your convenience, either scheduled or ad hoc.

Online meetings provide the same functionality as standard person-to-person communications such as sending IMs, sharing your desktop or a program, and even creating a whiteboard on which to jot down ideas. They are all great ways to collaborate

with individuals both in and out of your organization. Online meetings will also save you the hassle and time associated with booking a room for a meeting, or having to travel to other locations.

Another area in which online meetings can be useful is when you're finding it difficult to align schedules. For example, you need to meet with your manager for just a short while, but there doesn't seem to be a way to fit you in. Online meetings are great for quickly covering the set agenda and then moving on to your next appointment.

Create an online meeting

1 Start your Outlook app.

(continued on next page)

1

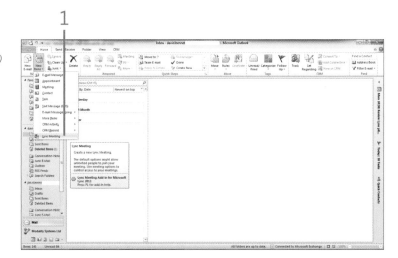

Create an online meeting *(continued)*

2 On the ribbon, click the Home tab. In the New group, click New Items and then, on the menu that appears, click Lync Meeting.

3 Insert the email addresses of the individuals whom you would like to attend the online meeting and then click Send.

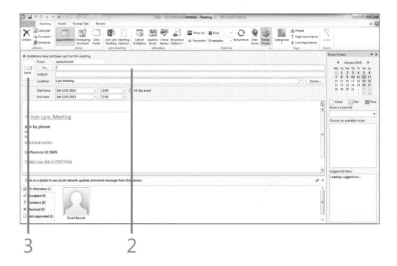

Viewing the Conversation History folder

The Conversation History folder contained within your Outlook account is a great feature with which you to review your history of communications with colleagues and coworkers. The type of conversations captured includes instant messages, incoming and outgoing telephone calls, and the conference calls you have joined. The information contained within the notifications can be extremely useful, providing names of those with whom you have communicated together with their contact details, which you can use to re-engage with them directly from within the notification.

View the Conversation History folder

1 In the Outlook Navigation pane, select the Conversation History folder.

2 Double-click the communication that you want to view.

3 The conversation is displayed in the main window.

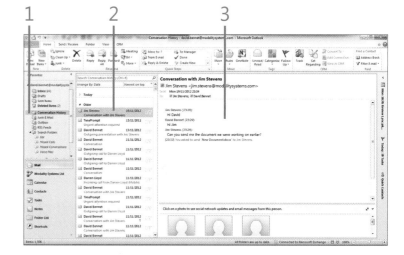

TIP A system administrator can activate or deactivate the Conversation History folder centrally or an individual user can do so by going into the Lync Options dialog box and clicking the Personal tab.

Viewing the Missed Conversations folder

The Missed Conversations folder contained within your Outlook account makes it possible for you to review the Lync 2013 conversations you have missed while otherwise engaged. The Missed Conversations folder records all missed instant messages and telephone calls, providing you with an easy to view breakdown of missed conversations, and the ability to re-engage with those who attempted to reach you without the need to switch to the Lync client.

View the Missed Conversation folder

1 In the Outlook Navigation pane, select the Missed Conversation folder.

2 Click the missed conversation that you want to view.

3 View the missed conversation in the main window.

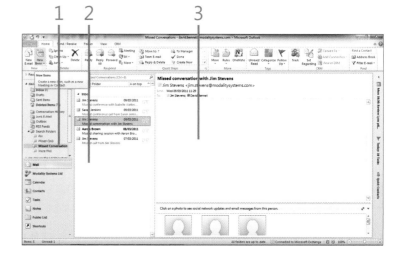

Viewing the Missed Calls folder

The Missed Calls folder operates in a similar fashion to that of the Missed Conversation folder, except the Missed Calls folder only registers the calls you have missed. The missed calls function provides you with an easy to navigate and searchable folder in which you can view just the telephone calls you have missed, saving you the time and effort otherwise spent trawling through the other forms of missed conversation such as IMs.

View the Missed Call folder

1 In the Outlook Navigation pane, select the Missed Calls folder.

2 Click the missed call that you want to view.

3 View the missed call in the main window.

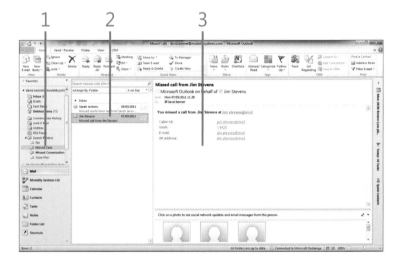

Viewing missed ad hoc conference calls

In addition to missed calls, the Missed Calls folder also lists the ad hoc (non-scheduled) conference calls that you have missed. These occur when two parties are already engaged on a call and want to invite you to their discussion, but for some reason, you are unable to answer. The missed conference calls function provides details of the conference call you missed together with a list of the attendees and their contact details.

View missed ad hoc conference calls

1 In the Outlook Navigation pane, select the Missed Calls folder.

2 Click the missed conference call.

3 View the missed conference call in the main window.

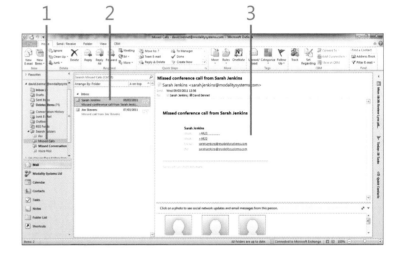

Configuring your privacy settings

Lync 2013 has been designed to provide your colleagues and coworkers with as much information about your availability as possible. By integrating with Outlook, Lync is able to inform them of the meetings you are attending and how long it will be until you are available again. This is a great feature for those colleagues with whom you work closely, but it might provide a little too much information to others.

With this in mind, you can configure certain relationship privacy settings in Lync so that you can provide all information relating to your availability to some colleagues and coworkers, and minimal information to others such as external contacts.

Configure your privacy settings

1 In the Lync client window, click the Search box and enter the name of the person for whom you want to change privacy settings.

2 Right-click the individual's contact card.

3 On the shortcut menu that appears, point to Change Privacy Relationship.

4 From the submenu that appears, select the most appropriate privacy setting.

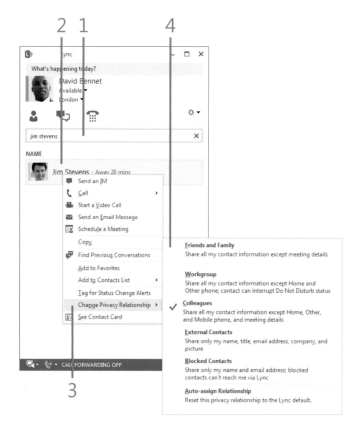

Accessing online meetings via the Lync Web App

I am frequently asked by customers whether colleagues and coworkers who don't have Lync can join an online meeting, and if so, how. This usually relates to contacts in external companies, but it can sometimes be members of the same organization who work in different departments, but don't have Lync.

In fact, the answer is yes, using the Lync 2013 Web App.

Access to the Lync Web App is provided automatically when a contact clicks the online meeting invite you sent them, and unlike previous versions of the Lync Web App provided in Lync 2010, The new version provides them with a feature-rich experience that includes audio, video, and full presentation capabilities equivalent to the desktop Lync 2013 client.

Access an online meeting via Lync Web App

1 From within your online meeting invitation in Outlook, click Join Lync Meeting.

(continued on next page)

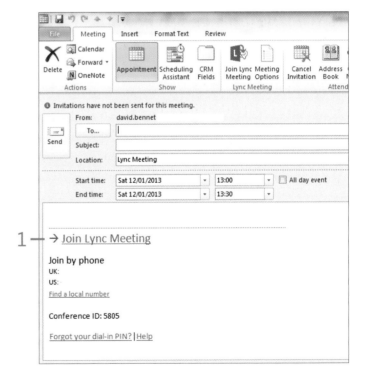

1—

TIP Depending on the meeting options set by the meeting organizer, you'll either enter the meeting right away or wait in the "meeting lobby" until admitted.

Access an online meeting via Lync Web App *(continued)*

2 On the Lync Web App Home page, type your name in the text box to sign in as a guest or click Sign In if you are from the organizer's company to enter your company credentials.

3 Ensure that you select the option to install the Lync Web App plug-in.

4 Click Join The Meeting.

5 You've now joined the online meeting.

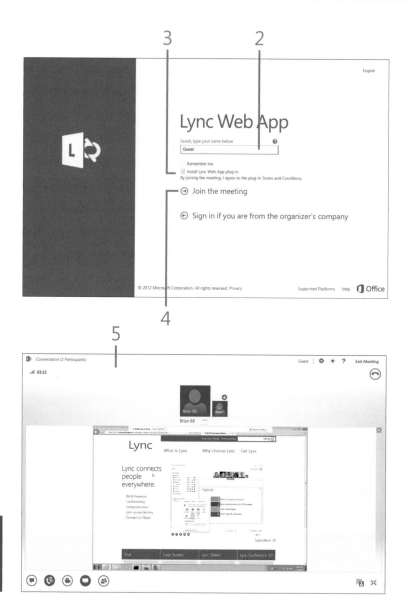

> **TIP** If you choose not to select the Install Lync Web-App plug-in and click to join the meeting, you'll be prompted to enter a phone number at which Lync can call you so that you can join the audio portion of the meeting on a different device.

Viewing Outlook Quick Contacts

As part of the Lync 2013 integration with Outlook, you are able to view the groups that you've created in Lync from within Outlook.

Each group that you have created within Lync will be replicated in Outlook, providing you with a quick an efficient way by which to initiate conversations, without the need to open your Lync client.

View Outlook Quick Contacts

1 In Outlook, right-click the pane at the right side of the window and then, on the shortcut menu that appears, click Quick Contacts.

2 Note your Lync Groups and associated users.

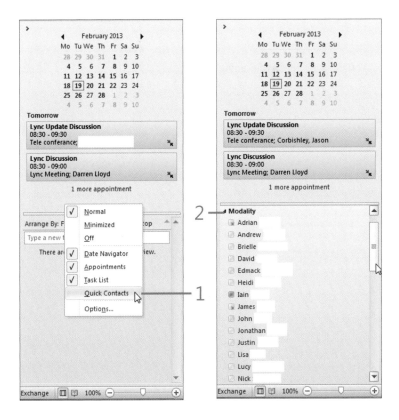

Using the Lync 2013 voice features

8

Microsoft Lync 2013 is a feature-rich, enterprise voice-telephony platform; or, in less regal-sounding terms, it does everything you would expect from a telephone system and a whole lot more.

When designing its telephony platform, Microsoft didn't rely on copying what had come before; instead, it took a fresh look at the way people communicate. By designing a platform with which individual users can configure their own communication environment, Microsoft has transformed the mundane world of telephony into an intuitive and productivity-led environment that compliments the way you work.

The key requirements of all telephony systems remain constant. The need to place calls, answer calls, forward calls, and place calls on hold hasn't changed, but what has changed is the way we now communicate with each other and the devices to which we have access. By integrating new features such as instant messaging and desktop sharing into our telephony environment and making these available across multiple devices including mobile phones and tablets, Lync 2013 has the ability to improve access to information and knowledge while at the same time making you more productive.

In this section:

- Making a telephone call
- Making a video call
- Managing an incoming call
- Forwarding an incoming call to voicemail
- Viewing and responding to a missed call
- Placing a call on hold
- Transferring a call
- Consultative transferring
- Calling a contact's voicemail
- Using the dial pad to navigate a call menu

Making a telephone call

Making a telephone call is quite clearly a key feature of any telephony system, but the process followed when making a call is not always a simple as you might think. For instance, when you call a colleague or coworker, you're normally required to enter his telephone or extension number. Now, for people you communicate with on a regular basis, this is not normally an issue, as you probably remember their contact details.

However, for those individuals whom you don't call regularly, the process of finding their contact details is often time-consuming and laborious. Searching for contact details on a directory on your company intranet site or even within a physical book is not uncommon, and if these are not updated at regular intervals, it can lead to frustration and annoyance. Imagine how much time you could save if you didn't have to look up a number.

To complicate matters—and again impact your productivity—when you make a call you can't always be guaranteed of an answer, and in these situations, you often find yourself trying repeatedly until at some point your call is answered. How very inconvenient.

In designing Lync 2013, Microsoft has removed the hassle associated with finding a number and then blind-calling individuals in the hope that they will answer. To call a contact you simply have to type his name and then click to initiate the call. Lync also apprises you of the availability of your contacts. In doing so, you can set your expectation as to whether they are available to answer your call, thus eliminating the time wasted calling someone who is not there.

Make a telephone call

1 In the Lync client window, in the Search box, type the name of the person whom you want to call.

2 Hover over the contact card to display the Quick Lync bar, which presents communications options (note their availability).

3 Click the Phone button.

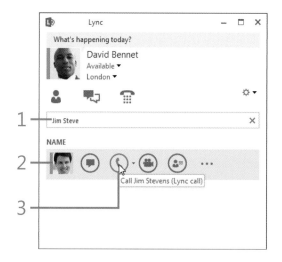

> ✓ **TIP** When you click the Phone button to initiate the call, depending on how your administrator has configured Lync's global default settings, Lync 2013 might call the last number dialed; for example, the contact's mobile phone. To select a different number, click the More Options button (the ellipsis to the right of the phone button).

Making a video call

The ability to make a video call is a great feature that Lync 2013 provides, because seeing the person you are speaking with often provides additional information as to how they are feeling, and also their reaction to what you are saying. Making a video call is straightforward, and Lync even provides you with information relating to whether the person you are calling is video-capable and able to participate in a video call.

Make a video call

1 In the Lync client window, in the Search box, type the name of the person with whom you to start a video call.

2 Hover over the contact card to display the Quick Lync bar.

  Note the contact's availability and video capability.

3 Click the Start Video button.

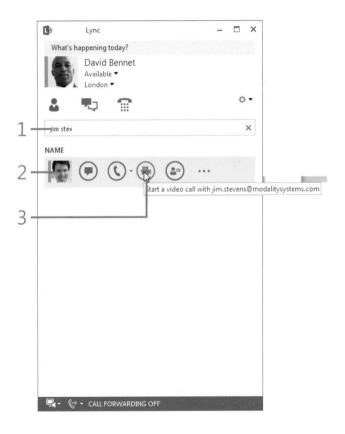

Managing an incoming call

Lync 2013 provides a couple of methods by which to answer an incoming call. The first, and probably the easiest, is to lift the handset of your desk phone if you have one. However, what if you don't have a desk phone and instead utilize a headset? In this instance, the easiest way to answer an incoming call is via the Incoming Call pop-up notification that Lync displays.

Answering the call in this manner is simple, but on those occasions when you're busy, Lync also provides you with the option to ignore the call or divert it to your voicemail facility, if you have one. Each is demonstrated here.

Answer an incoming call

1 Click the Incoming Call notification.

Forwarding an incoming call to voicemail

Occasionally, you might want to forward an incoming call directly to your voicemail. For example, you might be in the middle of a meeting and don't want to be disturbed. Choosing to forward the call to your voicemail provides the caller with the option of leaving you a message that you can listen to and act upon when you are free.

Forward and incoming call to voicemail

1 On the Incoming Call pop-up notification, click Options.

2 On the menu that appears, click Voice Mail.

TIP If you don't have voicemail, you can click Ignore on the Incoming Call pop-up notification.

TIP In addition to ringing your preferred number, you can configure Lync 2013 to simultaneously ring another number such as your cell phone. You can read more about this feature in Section 10, "Setting up your telephony environment."

Viewing and responding to a missed call

The missed call folder contained within your Outlook account is a great feature. With it, you can review all the calls you've missed in a quick and easy format.

The information contained within the notifications is intuitive and can be extremely useful, providing names and contact details of those who have attempted to call you so that you can call them back.

View and respond to a missed call

1 In Outlook, in the Folder pane, select the Missed Calls folder.

2 Select the missed call that you want to view.

3 If you want to call the individual, click the telephone number contained within the missed call email.

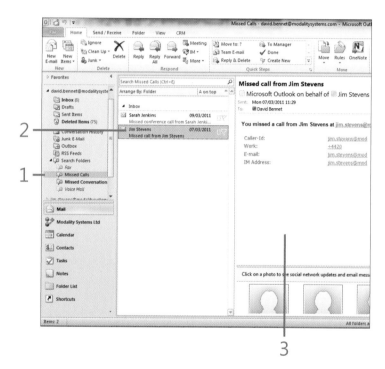

✓ **TIP** You can also view missed calls on the Conversation History tab from within the Lync 2013 client.

Placing a call on hold

There are times when you are on a call and you need to place the caller on hold while you momentarily attend to other tasks. You can do so with Lync 2013.

Place a call on hold

1 In an active conversation window, hover over the Phone button.

2 In the dialog box that opens, click Hold Call.

Transferring a call

There are a number of reasons why you might need to transfer a call. For example, maybe you have been asked a question for which you're unable to provide an answer, but you know a colleague who can assist. The ability to transfer a call is a standard requirement of any telephony platform, and it is particularly easy to do in Lync 2013.

Transfer a call

1   In an active conversation window, hover over the Phone button.

2   In the dialog box that opens, click Transfer Call.

3   Click Another Person Or Number.

(continued on next page)

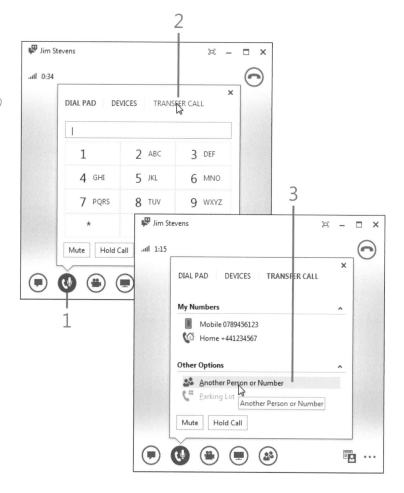

Transfer a call *(continued)*

4 In the main Lync client window, in the Search box, type the name of the individual to whom you want to transfer the call.

5 Double-click the contact card of the individual.

4 5

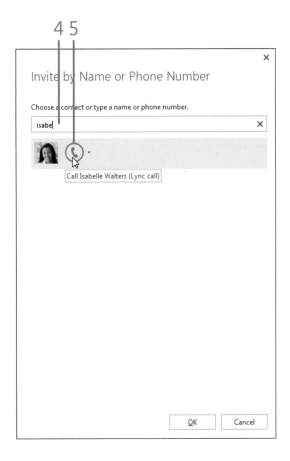

Invite by Name or Phone Number

Choose a contact or type a name or phone number.

isabe

Call Isabelle Walters (Lync call)

OK   Cancel

Consultative transferring

Sometimes, the ability to simply transfer a call is not enough, and out of courtesy, you might want to speak with the recipient of the transfer to inform that person of the incoming call. Consultative transfer, as it is known, is one of the very few functions in Lync 2013 that isn't as intuitive as you might expect; however, it's not terribly difficult, either, as you will see in the following task.

Consultative transfer

1 In an active conversation window, hover over the Phone button.

2 In the dialog box that opens, click Hold Call.

(continued on next page)

Consultative transfer *(continued)*

3 In the main Lync client window, in the Search box, type the name of the individual to whom you want to transfer the call.

4 Hover over that person's contact card to display the Quick Lync bar and then click the Call button.

(continued on next page)

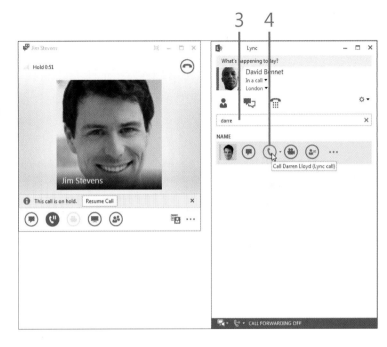

Consultative transfer (continued)

5 Return to the original call that is on hold and hover over the Hold button.

6 Click the name of the individual contained within the Current Conversation section to transfer the call.

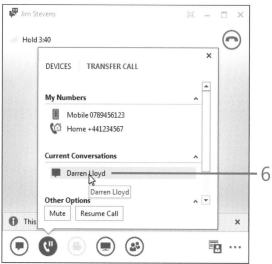

Calling a contact's voicemail

You're late for a meeting, but you need to provide a colleague with a quick update about a piece of work you are completing together. You'd love to be able to speak directly with her, but you don't have the time for a prolonged conversation. For scenarios such as this, Lync 2013 gives you the ability to call your colleague's voicemail directly so that you can leave a message and then get on to your other business.

Call a contact's voicemail

1 In the Lync client window, click the search box and enter the name of the person to whom you want to to call.

2 Hover over that person's contact card to display the Quick Lync bar.

3 Click the ellipsis to the right of the phone icon, and from the menu that appears, select Voice Mail.

> **TIP** The ability to call a contact's voicemail is a feature that needs to be configured by a systems administrator. If this functionality is not enabled by the administrator, you will not be able to do this.

Using the dial pad to navigate a call menu

When using Lync 2013 to make a call, you might on occasion find yourself forwarded to a switchboard from which you need to navigate a menu system to direct your call to its destination.

You can accomplish this in many ways, including using the dial pad on your desk phone, but if you're using a headset, you can also use the dial pad.

Use the dial pad to navigate a call menu

1 In an active conversation window, click the Phone button.

2 In the dialog box that opens, click Dial Pad and then click the number relating to the option you require from the audio-driven menu choices.

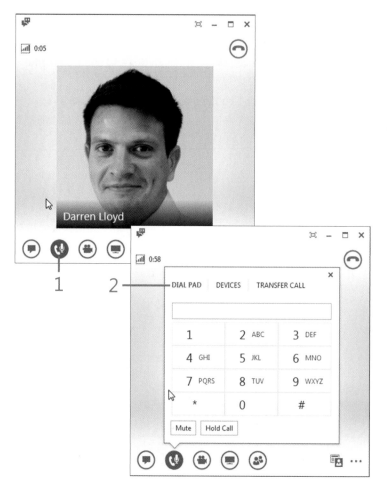

Using Lync as your phone

9

To achieve the best experience with your telephony environment and so that you can become more productive, Microsoft Lync 2013 provides you with a number of options related to the types of devices, ringtones, and sounds that you can configure within your personal settings. Furthermore, Microsoft has also made it possible for you to configure additional contact details, beyond the default settings, and the option to display these on your contact card when viewed by others.

Microsoft's approach to the configuration of your telephony environment has been to provide the user with as much flexibility as possible in determining how it functions, and in this section, I'll demonstrate how to set up your basic environment. You can find details on configuring the more advanced functions such as call forwarding and simultaneous ringing in Section 10, "Setting up your telephony environment."

In this section:

- Adding or editing additional telephone numbers
- Setting your primary audio device
- Setting a secondary ringer
- Checking primary audio device call quality
- Setting ringtones and sounds

Adding or editing additional telephone numbers

Lync 2013 draws the majority of your contact information from a central store that is managed and updated by your IT department. The type of information included consists of various telephone numbers; for example, your work and mobile numbers as well as your email address. Sometimes, though, you might want to add an additional number at which your colleagues and coworkers can reach you.

Add or edit additional telephone numbers

1   In the Lync client window, click the Settings icon (the small gear graphic).

2   In the Options dialog box, click the Phones tab.

3   Click Home Phone or Other Phone.

4   In the Edit Phone Number dialog box, type the new number in the text box and then click OK.

(continued on next page)

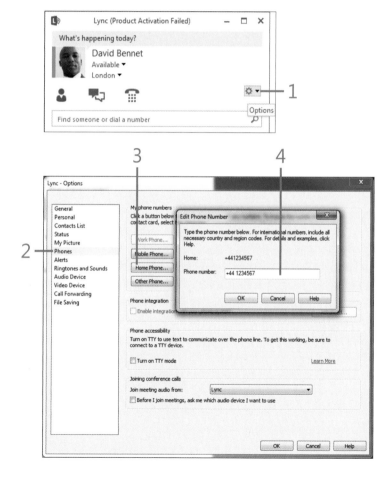

Add or edit additional telephone numbers *(continued)*

5   Select the Include In My Contact Card check box.

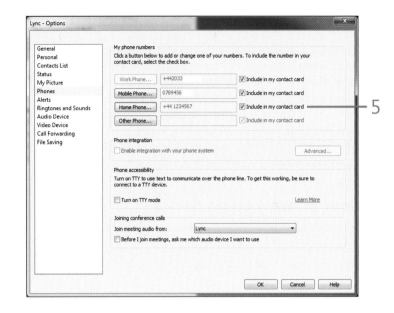

Setting your primary audio device

With Lync 2013, you can use a number of different telephony endpoints when making or receiving calls or, indeed, when participating in conference calls. The wide range of devices offers convenience and flexibility such that when you are working from home or a coffee shop, you might choose to use a headset; while working from the office, you might prefer to use a desk phone. Additionally, you have the option to use a speaker phone when attending a conference call.

With the range of endpoints available, Lync has made it easy for you to switch between devices—even during a call—so that when you receive or make a call, you can choose to use the device that's most appropriate for your environment. In addition, you can also set the audio levels of the device you choose to use, including the speaker, microphone, and ringer levels.

Set your primary audio device

1 In the Lync client window, click the Settings icon (the small gear graphic).

(continued on next page)

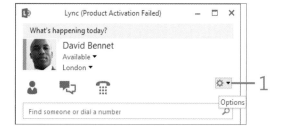

✓ **TIP**   You can also select your primary audio device by clicking the device icon in the lower-left corner of your Lync 2013 client. Also, you can switch devices while in a call without the call disconnecting.

Set your primary audio device *(continued)*

2 In the Options dialog box, click the Audio Device tab.

3 In the Select The Device You Want To Use For Audio Calls list box, click a device.

4 Adjust the speaker, microphone, and ringer levels to suit your preference and click OK.

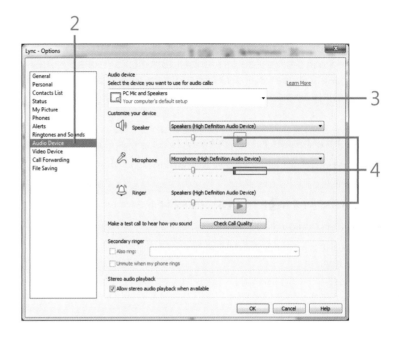

Setting a secondary ringer

In addition to selecting the audio device you prefer, with Lync 2013, you can set a secondary ringer, as well. For example, you can choose to have your desktop speakers ring in addition to your primary audio device. This can be quite a useful feature when you are using a headset, because without the secondary ringer, the only way you will be aware of an incoming call is via the Incoming Call pop-up notification.

Set a secondary ringer

1   In the Lync client window, click the Settings icon (the small gear graphic).

2   In the Options dialog box, click the Audio Device tab.

3   In the Secondary Ringer section, select the Also Ring check box.

4   In the list box, select the device that you want to use as the secondary ringer.

5   Click OK.

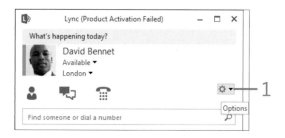

Checking primary audio device call quality

After you've selected your primary audio device, Lync 2013 provides you with the ability to check the quality of the call experience when using your preferred device. By making a test call, Lync 2013 will play back the audio from the test so that you can hear for yourself the quality of the audio experienced by colleagues and coworkers when communicating with you.

Check call quality

1 In the Lync client window, click the Settings icon (the small gear graphic).

2 In the Options dialog box, click the Audio Device tab.

3 Click Check Call Quality button.

(continued on next page)

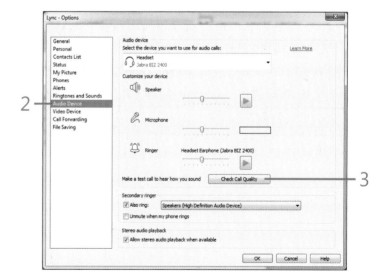

TIP You can also complete this task by clicking the Phone button within your Lync 2013 client and selecting Check.

Check call quality *(continued)*

4 Follow the audio instructions from within the Audio Test Service asking you to record a message. After you've recorded a sample message, Lync will play the message back to you.

4

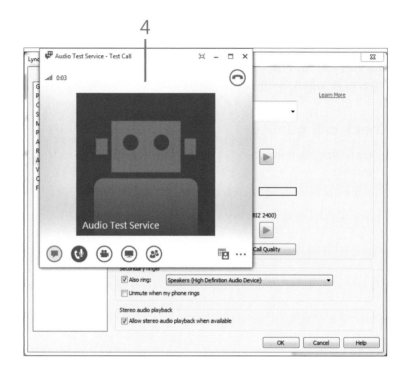

Setting ringtones and sounds

With Lync 2013, you can select from a number of preconfigured ringtones and assign them to particular forms of incoming calls. For example, you can set up a specific ringtone for standard incoming Lync calls, another ringtone for team call groups, one for delegate groups, and another for response groups. The ability to assign different ringtones to specific incoming call types gives you an indication of who's calling and why.

Set ringtones and sounds

1 In the Lync client window, click the Settings icon (the small gear graphic).

2 In the Options dialog box, click the Ringtones And Sounds tab.

3 In the Ringtones section, select the type of incoming call.

4 Browse the available list of ringtones until you find your preferred option.

5 Repeat steps 3 and 4 for all types of call and then click OK.

Setting up your telephony environment

10

To make it possible for you to become more productive within your working environment, Microsoft has designed Lync 2013 to be as intuitive to use a possible. Lync gives you the ability to create your own telephony environment in which you dictate how incoming calls are handled, such as configuring what happens to a call when you are busy or away from the office.

The ability to configure your own unique telephony environment is a far cry from the types of telephony systems to which you might be accustomed. No longer do you have to liaise with your IT or communications department to set up *hunt groups* or call *pickup groups*, because you now have the ability to create your own custom environment in a matter of minutes.

Lync makes it easy to configure, test, and deploy your own communications environment, meaning if you need to change it because you are not entirely happy with the way it functions, you can quickly start again and implement a model that best meets your requirements.

In this section:

- Setting up call forwarding
- Setting up simultaneous ringing
- Setting up a team-call group
- Setting up a delegate
- Changing how unanswered calls are managed

Setting up call forwarding

The process of creating and viewing your call forwarding settings in Lync 2013 is straightforward, and you are provided with the option of forwarding calls to a new number or contact, a mobile phone, a delegate, or indeed, straight to your voicemail.

An overview of your current settings and an example of what will happen to incoming calls is always provided in the setup menu, so at a glance it's easy to understand how you have your call routing environment configured.

Set up call forwarding

1 At the bottom of the Lync client window, click the Call Forward Options button.

2 On the menu that appears, click Call Forwarding Settings.

(continued on next page)

Set up call forwarding *(continued)*

3

3 In the Options dialog box, click the Call Forwarding tab and then, in the Call Forwarding section, click Forward My Calls To.

4 In the list box, select New Number Or Contract.

5 In the Forward Calls window, type the name of the contact or telephone number and then click OK.

6 Note the Current Call Forwarding settings displayed in the main window.

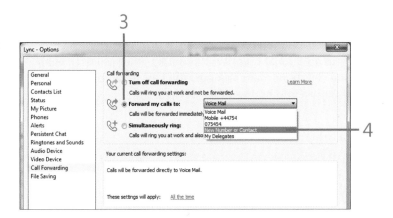

4

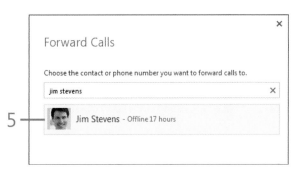

5

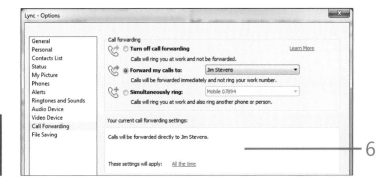

6

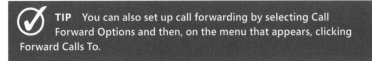

TIP You can also set up call forwarding by selecting Call Forward Options and then, on the menu that appears, clicking Forward Calls To.

Setting up simultaneous ringing

Simultaneous ring is a great Lync 2013 feature by which you can set up additional numbers or contacts that will ring when someone calls your main number. You can set an option to add a delay before ringing the other devices.

This feature is great when you're moving around the office and want to redirect calls to your mobile phone or when you're working in a busy office and want to distribute your incoming calls among your team.

There are many ways in which simultaneous ring can be used, and I cover them all on the following pages.

Set up simultaneous ringing

1 At the bottom of the Lync client window, click the Call Forward Options button.

2 On the menu that appears, click Call Forwarding Settings.

(continued on next page)

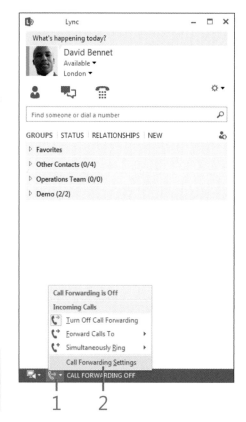

> ✓ **TIP** You can also set up simultaneous ring by selecting Call Forward Options and then, on the menu that appears, clicking Simultaneously Ring.

Set up simultaneous ringing (continued)

3 In the Options dialog box, click the Call Forwarding tab and then, in the Call Forwarding section, click Simultaneous Ring.

4 In the list box, select New Number.

5 In the Edit Phone Number dialog box, type the new number and click OK.

6 Observe that the current simultaneous ring settings are displayed in the main window.

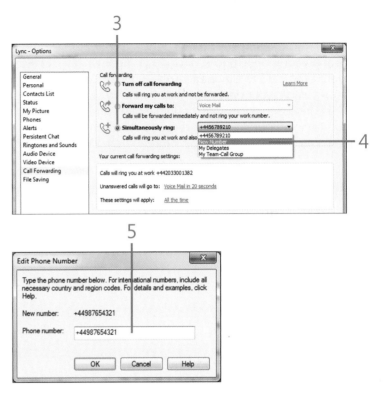

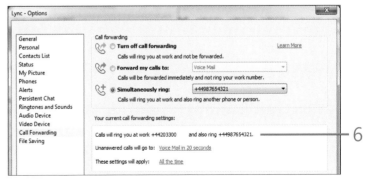

> **TIP** Any personal numbers unique to yourself that have been entered by the system administrator appear by default as a possible selection in the Simultaneously Ring list box in the Options dialog box.

Setting up a team-call group

In addition to simultaneous ringing between your primary audio device and your mobile phone or another number, you can also configure Lync 2013 to simultaneously ring your Lync-enabled colleagues within your department or team. You can create team-call groups to encompass multiple members of your team, and you can configure it so that they are called simultaneously when you receive an inbound call, or after a specified delay.

An overview of your current settings and an example of what will happen to incoming calls is always provided in the setup menu.

Set up a team-call group

1 At the bottom of the Lync client window, click the Call Forward Options button.

2 On the menu that appears, click Call Forwarding Settings.

(continued on next page)

Set up a team-call group *(continued)*

3 In the Options dialog box, click the Call Forwarding tab and then, in the Call Forwarding section, click Simultaneous Ring.

4 In the list box, select My Team-Call Group.

5 In the Call Forwarding – Team-Call Group dialog box, click Add.

(continued on next page)

3

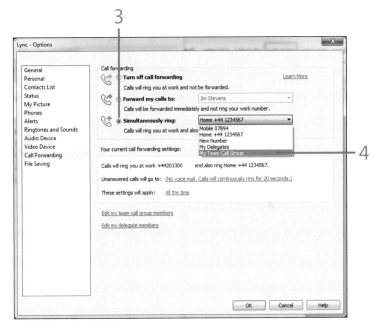

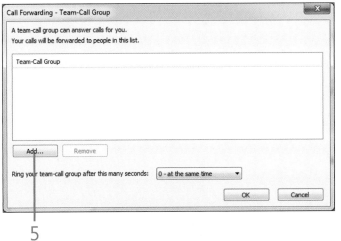

5

Set up a team-call group *(continued)*

6 Type the names of the colleague you wish to add to your team call group and click OK.

7 Click the Ring Your Team-Call Group After This Many Seconds list box and select the delay.

8 Click OK.

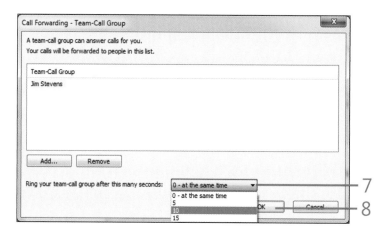

✓ **TIP** When you configure a new team-call group, a new group called Team-Call Group is added to your contact groups in the main window of your Lync 2013 client.

Setting up a delegate

Lync 2013 gives you the option to configure delegates who can make and receive calls on your behalf. This is ideally suited to those of you who have personal assistants or, indeed, receive calls on behalf of your line manager or supervisor.

Set up a delegate

1 At the bottom of the Lync client window, click the Call Forward Options button.

2 On the menu that appears, click Call Forwarding Settings.

(continued on next page)

Set up a delegate (continued)

3 In the Options dialog box, click the Call Forwarding tab and then, in the Call Forwarding section, click Simultaneous Ring.

4 In the list box, select My Delegates.

5 In the Call Forwarding – Delegates dialog box, click Add.

(continued on next page)

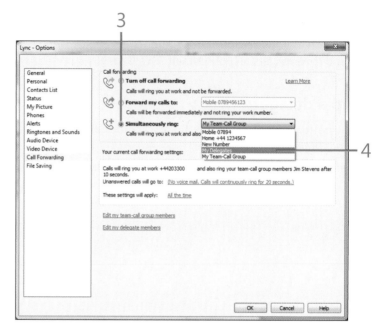

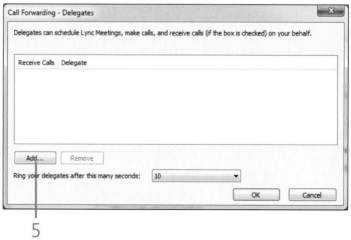

Set up a delegate *(continued)*

6 In the Choose A Delegate dialog box, type the name of the contact that you want to add as a delegate and then click OK.

(continued on next page)

Set up a delegate *(continued)*

7 Back in the Call Forwarding – Delegates dialog box, click the Ring Your Delegates After This Many Seconds list box and select the delay.

8 Click OK.

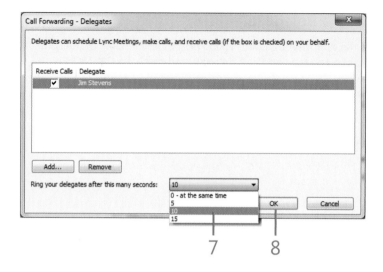

Changing how unanswered calls are managed

Lync 2013 makes it easy for you to view and edit how your incoming calls are managed and also what happens to them when you are away from your desk or office. But what about unanswered calls?

Viewing and configuring what happens to calls that you don't answer is pretty simple. Lync displays your settings information in the main window, and it's from within this window that you are able to modify your configurations.

Change how unanswered calls are managed

1 At the bottom of the Lync client window, click the Call Forward Options button.

2 On the menu that appears, click Call Forwarding Settings.

(continued on next page)

Change how unanswered calls are managed *(continued)*

3 In the Options dialog box, click the Call Forwarding tab and then, in the Your Current Call Forwarding Settings section, click the link adjacent to Unanswered Calls Will Go To.

4 In the Call Forwarding – Unanswered Calls dialog box, in the list box, select the option you require.

5 Click the Ring For This Many Seconds Before Redirecting list box and select the delay. Click OK.

6 Note your new current call forwarding settings.

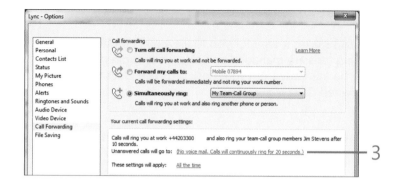

3

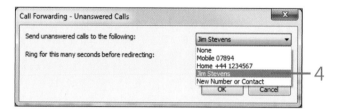

4

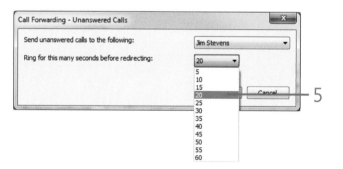

5

6

✓ **TIP**   Lync 2013 is able to identify whether you have a voicemail account set up. If you do not have a voicemail account, the option to forward to voicemail will not be provided in the menu.

Reviewing your voicemail from within Microsoft Outlook

11

Voicemail is a key requirement of any enterprise-grade telephony system, but over the years, the features offered by voicemail systems have advanced very little. The ability to change your internal and external greetings is about as much as any voicemail system has been able to offer. At the same time, the ability to integrate with your desktop has been either non-existent or, at best, cumbersome and difficult to use.

The voicemail features provided by Microsoft Exchange are a world apart from anything you might have used in the past. Features such as *unified messaging* whereby your voicemail appears in your Outlook Inbox, and the option to have new emails and calendar entries read back to you are all standard features within Exchange. All of them work to provide you with a voicemail system that is functional and intuitive, while improving your productivity like no other.

Welcome to a new age of voicemail functionality!

In this section:

- Listening to your voicemail
- Calling your voicemail and auto attendant
- Sending an "I'll be late" notification
- Changing your voicemail greeting
- Forwarding your voicemail

Listening to your voicemail

Lync 2013 provides you with numerous methods by which you can listen to your voicemail, both directly from your Lync 2013 client and from within Outlook. I cover each of these options in order so that you can select the method that best suits the way you work to make you most productive.

Listen to your voicemail (Lync client)

1 In the Lync client window, click the Phone button.

2 Hover over the voicemail to which you want to listen.

3 Select the Play button.

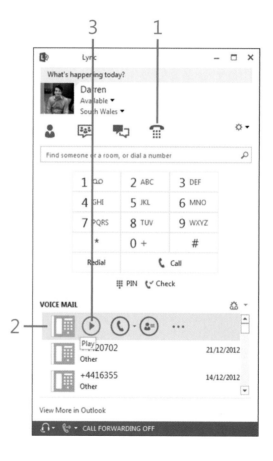

Listen to your voicemail in Outlook

1 In Outlook, in the Folder pane, click the Search Folders item.

2 Select the Voice Mail folder.

3 In the Inbox, select the voicemail to which you want to listen.

4 In the Reading pane, click the Play button.

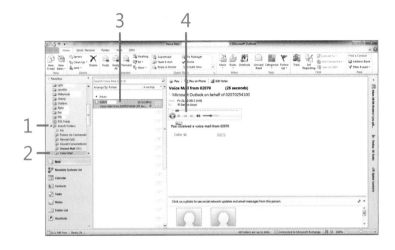

 TIP If you are in a public area and do not want people listening to your voicemail when you play it, either insert your headphones or, at the top of the email message containing the voicemail, click the Play On Phone option. You'll then be prompted to enter a number, for instance your mobile, to which to direct the voicemail.

 TIP As well as being saved in the Voicemail folder within Outlook, your voicemails also appear in your Inbox by default.

Calling your voicemail and auto attendant

In addition to being able to retrieve and listen to your voicemail in both Lync 2013 and Outlook, you can also call your voice-mail. When calling your voicemail, you are greeted by an auto attendant that guides you to it (by using voice commands or the keypad, if you so prefer).

In addition to voicemail, the Exchange auto attendant can also access your personal email and calendar, providing you with the ability to have your emails read back to you, and also informing you of the meetings you have in your calendar on any specific date.

Call your voicemail

1 In the Lync client window, click the Phone button.

2 Toward the bottom of the window, above the list of voicemails, click the Voicemail Settings button (the graphic that looks like half a gear over a cassette tape).

3 On the menu that appears, click Call Voice Mail.

(continued on next page)

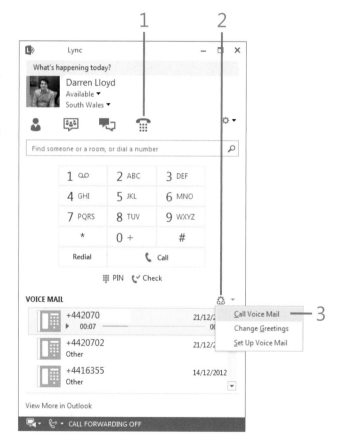

Call your voicemail (continued)

4 Follow the audio instructions and then, when prompted, say "Voicemail."

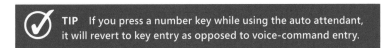

TIP If you press a number key while using the auto attendant, it will revert to key entry as opposed to voice-command entry.

Access your email from the auto attendant

1 In the Lync client window, click the Phone button.

2 Toward the bottom of the window, above the list of voicemails, click the Voicemail Settings button.

3 On the menu that appears, click Call Voice Mail.

(continued on next page)

Access your email from the auto attendant *(continued)*

4 Follow the audio instructions and then, when prompted, say "Email."

Access your calendar from the auto attendant

1 In the Lync client window, click the Phone button.

2 Toward the bottom of the window, above the list of voicemails, click the Voicemail Settings button.

3 On the menu that appears, click Call Voice Mail.

(continued on next page)

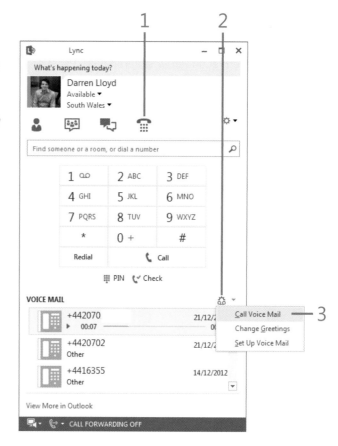

Access your calendar from the auto attendant *(continued)*

4 Follow the audio instructions and then, when prompted, say "Calendar."

Sending an "I'll be late" notification

Having left in plenty of time for a meeting at one of your branch offices, suddenly you're faced with traffic, and it looks like you're going to be a little late. You've tried calling your colleagues to inform them, but they're not answering their phones. If there's any good news in this scenario, it's that Lync 2013 provides you with a new way for you to update them.

Voice commands form an integral feature of the Lync 2013 voicemail functionality, and when accessing your calendar via the auto attendant, you can send an "I'll be late" message to the attendees of a meeting, notifying them that you are running late. By following the prompts and issuing your own voice commands, you're even able to let the attendees know how long you think you will be delayed.

Send an "I'll be late" notification

1 In the Lync client window, click the Phone button.

2 Toward the bottom of the window, above the list of voicemails, click the Voicemail Settings button.

3 On the menu that appears, click Call Voice Mail.

(continued on next page)

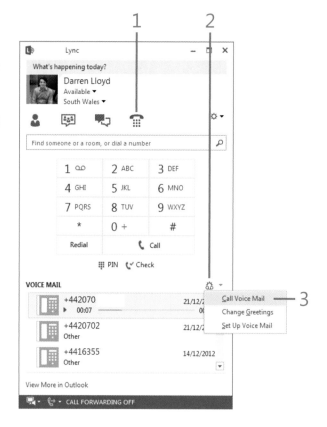

Send an "I'll be late" notification *(continued)*

4 Follow the audio instructions and then, when prompted, say "Calendar." When prompted, state the date that you wish to open, followed by the voice command "send an I'll be late message." Continue to follow the voice prompts until the process is complete.

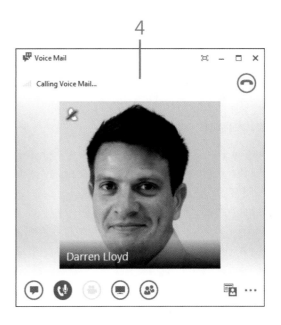

Changing your voicemail greeting

Changing your voicemail greeting in Lync 2013 is a straightforward task. You can record and playback your greeting until you are comfortable with it being published, giving you the peace of mind that your greeting is both informative and professional for those who are trying to call you.

Change your voicemail greeting

1 In the Lync client window, click the Phone button.

2 Toward the bottom of the window, above the list of voicemails, click the Voicemail Settings button.

3 On the menu that appears, click Change Greetings.

(continued on next page)

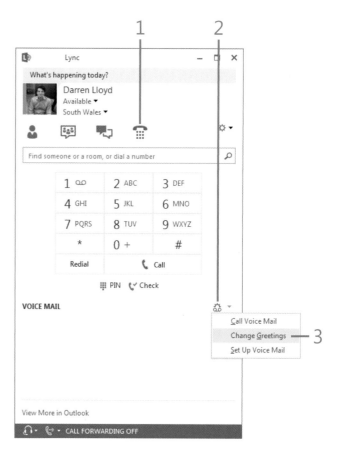

Change your voicemail greeting *(continued)*

4 Follow the audio instructions and then press 2 to record your new greeting.

Forwarding your voicemail

The ability to forward your voicemail to another colleague or coworker is a great feature provided with via Lync's integration with Outlook.

In the past, I've received voicemails that should in fact have been left with someone else or perhaps someone more capable of answering whatever query was contained within the message. After listening to the message numerous times to write down the caller's name and number, I would then make a note of the query, and either call or send an email to a colleague, asking him to follow it up.

Needless to say, this was both time-consuming and unproductive in equal measure.

Lync 2013 doesn't stop people from leaving you messages that would be better targeted at someone else within your organization, but what it can do via its integration with Outlook is forward the voicemail in a quick and efficient manner by email.

Forward your voicemail

1   In Outlook, in the Folder pane, click the Search Folders item.

2   Select the Voice Mail folder.

3   In the Inbox, select the voicemail that you want to forward.

4   On the ribbon, click the Home tab. In the Respond group, click Forward.

(continued on next page)

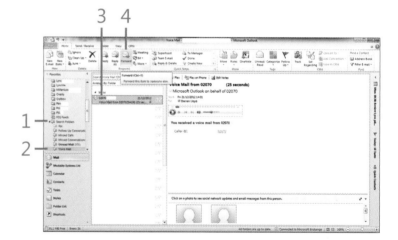

Forward your voicemail (continued)

5 In the new email message that opens, type the name of the recipient.

6 Click Send.

6 5

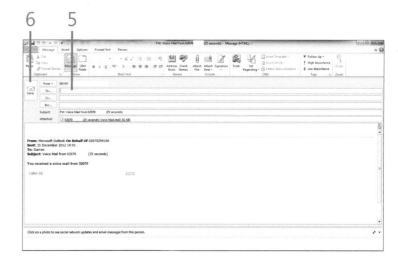

> **TIP** When forwarding the voicemail from within Outlook, you can treat it like any other email and add a note to inform the recipient why you are forwarding the email to them.

Taking advantage of Lync online meetings

12

Creating an online meeting is one of the most productive and time saving features offered by Microsoft Lync 2013. Online meetings can help increase meeting attendance, and in doing so, they can increase productivity for both yourself and your organization.

By removing the need to travel to and from meetings, online meetings significantly increase the window of opportunity for colleagues to attend.

Imagine you've just completed a meeting at a branch office, and now you need to be at another meeting across town. In all likelihood, if you didn't have Lync, you would not have accepted the meeting invite in the first place. However, by having access to Lync, you now have numerous options by which to join both meetings. For example, you could remain at the branch office and join via your corporate network, go to a local coffee shop and join via the shop's Wi-Fi, or you might choose to head back to your own office and join the meeting via audio on your mobile phone while travelling. All the while, you can still enjoy the same collaborative experience as if you were attending the meeting in person.

In this section:

- Scheduling an online meeting
- Joining an online meeting
- Enabling presenters
- Adding participants to meetings already in progress
- Muting participants
- Recording an online meeting
- Changing where your shared files or Lync recordings are saved

Scheduling an online meeting

The online meeting is an incredibly important feature within your unified communications toolbox, and one that when used correctly has the ability to vastly improve your productivity by reducing the time and effort required to attend meetings. Online meetings also have the potential to save your organization a considerable amount of money by reducing the traditional costs associated with attending meetings, such as travel and accommodation expenses.

In a world where time is money, and where the inability to easily agree to a mutually convenient time and place to schedule a meeting is common place, the online meeting provides an environment that encourages participation, and provides you with the opportunity to collaborate and progress important tasks in a more timely and productive manner.

Online meetings provide the same functionality as standard person-to-person communications, such as sending instant messages, sharing your desktop or a program, or even creating a white board in which to jot down ideas. They are a great way to collaborate with colleagues and coworkers. Online meetings will also save you the hassle and time associated with booking a room for a meeting or having to travel to other locations, and in doing so provide you with more time to focus on other tasks you are working on.

Another area in which online meetings can be useful is when you're finding it difficult to align schedules. For example, you need just 15 minutes of your manager's time, but there just doesn't seem to be a way to fit you in. Online meetings are great for quickly covering the set agenda and then moving on to your next appointment.

Schedule an online meeting

1 Open Microsoft Outlook.

2 On the ribbon, click the Home tab. In the New group, click New Items and then, on the menu, click Lync Meeting.

(continued on next page)

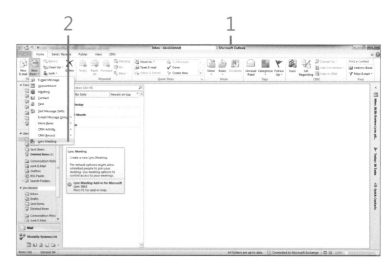

Schedule an online meeting *(continued)*

3 Insert the email address of the individuals you would like to attend the online meeting and click Send.

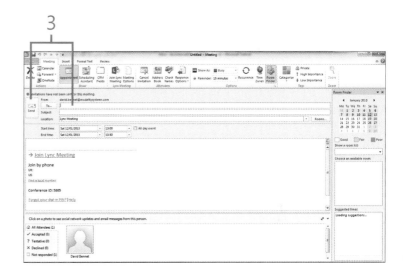

Joining an online meeting

The ease by which individuals are able to join an online meeting is crucial to their success and the overall adoption of this feature across your organization. Lync 2013 provides a number of methods by which to join an online meeting, including via your Lync client. Having joined a meeting, you can participate in a feature-rich environment that incorporates voice, video, and content sharing. You can also join via a mobile device that provides audio only. Whichever method you select, the process to join a meeting is straightforward.

Join an online meeting via your Lync 2013 client

1 In Microsoft Outlook, click Calendar.

2 Double-click the online meeting that you want to join.

3 Click Join Online Meeting.

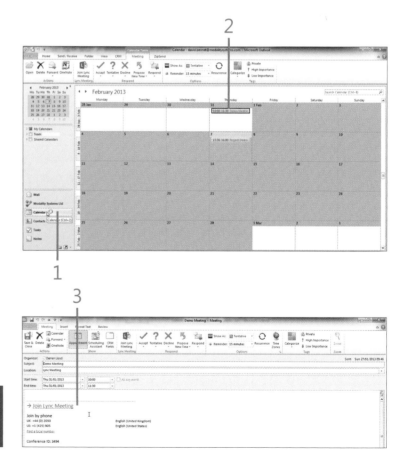

Join an online meeting via a mobile phone

1 In Microsoft Outlook, click Calendar.

2 Double-click the online meeting that you want to join.

3 Take note of the Join By Phone telephone number and Conference ID.

4 Using your mobile phone, call the Join By Phone number and then, when prompted, enter the Conference ID.

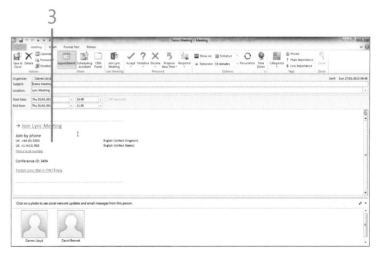

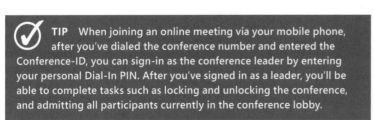

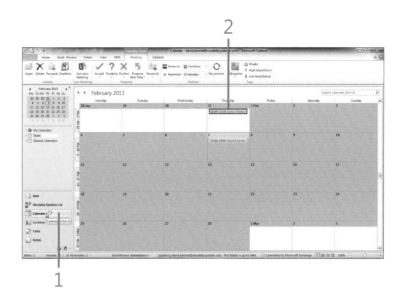

TIP When joining an online meeting via your mobile phone, after you've dialed the conference number and entered the Conference-ID, you can sign-in as the conference leader by entering your personal Dial-In PIN. After you've signed in as a leader, you'll be able to complete tasks such as locking and unlocking the conference, and admitting all participants currently in the conference lobby.

Enabling presenters

An important aspect of any meeting, whether it is face-to-face or online, is for all participants to contribute. Often, this can take the form of a report or document that has been prepared in advance and shared among attendees. The ability to communicate, share, and collaborate with others during an online meeting is key to ensuring a successful outcome, and with this in mind, Lync 2013 provides the meeting organizer with the ability to administer who is able to present material during individual sessions. This can be configured either when creating the online meeting environment itself or while the meeting is in progress. Both options are detailed in the following tasks.

Enable presenters during setup

1 In Outlook, on the Home tab, in the New group, click New Items and then, on the menu that appears, click Lync Meeting.

(continued on next page)

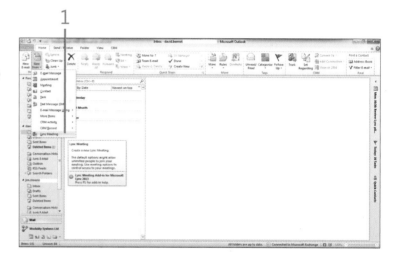

Enable presenters during setup *(continued)*

2 On the Meeting tab, in the Lync Meeting group, click Meeting Options.

3 To change the default meeting options, In the Lync Meeting Options dialog box, in the Where Do You Want To Meet Online section, click A New Meeting Space.

4 In the Who's A Presenter section, click the list box and select the type of attendee who is authorized to present.

5 Click OK.

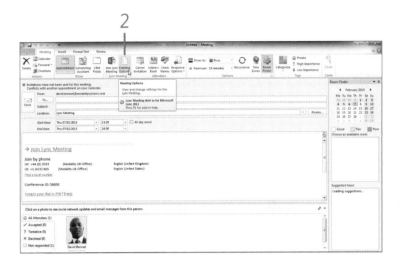

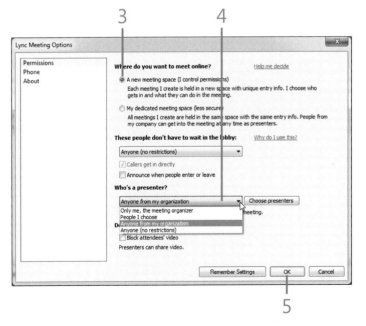

 TIP To save the settings for all new online meetings, click Remember Settings.

 TIP The option to enable presenters when you set up an online meeting might be disabled by the systems administrator.

Enable presenters during meeting

1 In the Conversations window, right-click the participant whom you want to enable as a presenter.

2 On the shortcut menu that appears, click Make A Presenter.

Adding participants to meetings already in progress

You have probably attended meetings during which a question was posed for which none of the participants knew the answer. This used to mean that you had to assign a colleague or coworker to the task of following up the query and reporting back during another meeting. This is both time-consuming, and in the scheme of things, unproductive.

Wouldn't it be great if you could check the availability of the person who might be able to assist with the query and then

immediately add her to the online meeting? Well, in Lync 2013 you can do just that, and there are a number of ways to do it, including sending the individual an email with the meeting invite or by simply adding her into the existing conference call via the Lync 2013 client.

The ability to add additional participants to an online meeting can remove bottlenecks to decision-making processes, and as a result, improve the productivity of your organization.

Add participants via email

1   In the Conversation window of an active online meeting, click the Participants button.

2   In the dialog box that opens, click the Actions tab.

3   Click Invite By Email.

Add participants from the Lync client

1 Open your Lync 2013 client.

2 Search for the colleague or coworker whom you want to add to the meeting.

3 If that person is available, drag their contact card into the existing online meeting window.

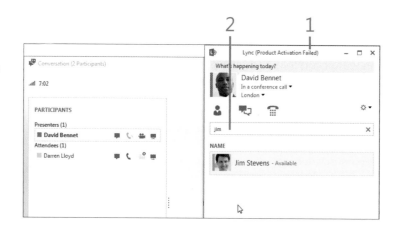

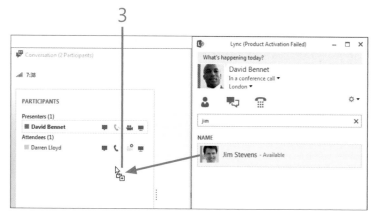

> ✓ **TIP** You can also add individuals to an existing online meeting by calling them at the number they have provided; for example, their mobile phone.

Muting participants

The ability to provide participants of an online meeting with an environment that is both functional and provides an experience that encourages participation and productivity is vital to the degree to which online meetings will be adopted across your organization. Two important elements of any successful and productive online meeting is the quality of the audio experience for all participants and reducing the background noise that can often occur if participants work in a noisy environment (or are not familiar with conference etiquette).

To manage the audio quality of an online meeting, Lync 2013 gives you the ability to mute participants during the meeting. This doesn't mean that participants are always muted; it simply means that the meeting organizer has the ability to manage the environment by muting individuals or all participants, as and when required.

Mute participants

1 In the Conversation window of an active online meeting, click the Participants button.

2 In the dialog box that opens, click the Actions tab and then click Mute Audience.

(continued on next page)

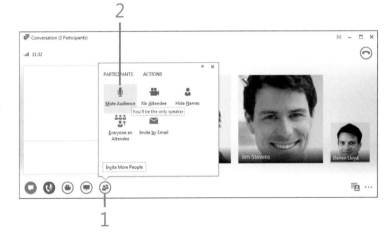

Mute participants *(continued)*

3 A pop-up message box appears in the attendees' windows, stating that the presenter has muted them.

3

Recording an online meeting

Recording Lync 2013 online meetings is a particularly useful feature with which you to view the content of individual meetings as and when required. It also gives colleagues and coworkers who were unable to attend a meeting an opportunity to view its content to bring them up to speed.

When recording an online meeting, Lync records all audio, video, instant messages, and shared content, providing those viewing it with an information-rich experience.

Record an online meeting

1 In the Conversation window of an active online meeting, click the More Options button (the ellipsis).

2 On the menu that appears, click the Start Recording command.

(continued on next page)

Record an online meeting *(continued)*

3 Participants are notified that the meeting is being recorded.

When you end the online meeting, the recording is managed by the Microsoft Lync Recording Manager.

4 Click Play to view the meeting content.

5 Click Publish to save to your meeting to a location where others can view it.

Changing where your shared files or Lync recordings are saved

The ability to save online meeting recordings is a great feature provided within the Lync 2013 client. To eliminate the chore of manually selecting the folder in which to store the recordings, you can set a default folder.

By default, Lync saves received files or Lync recordings to the following locations:

C:\Users\[username]\Documents\ My Received Files

Or

C:\Users\[username]\Videos\Lync Recordings

Change where shared files and Lync recordings are saved

1 In the Lync client window, click the Settings icon (the small gear graphic).

(continued on next page)

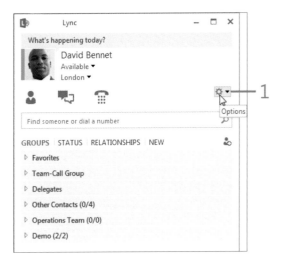

Change where shared files and Lync recordings are saved *(continued)*

2 In the Options dialog box, click the File Saving tab.

3 Change the location of either your File Transfers or Lync Recordings by clicking the respective browse button and then selecting the new location.

4 Click OK.

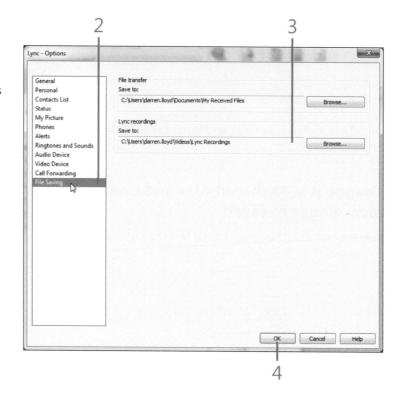

Using Lync persistent chat

13

Persistent chat is a new feature provided within the Microsoft Lync 2013 client that brings together dispersed members of your organization to work on specific projects to which their individual skills apply. By providing a single topic-based instant messaging environment, persistent chat rooms are a quick and efficient resource that encourages collaboration and participation, and in so doing, increases the productivity of its members.

Messages contained within each chat room remain there for predefined amount of time that you can configure. And, you can set up a moderator for each room to ensure its appropriate use.

Being a member of a room makes it possible for you to post updates, but you also have the ability to follow specific chat rooms made available to a global audience of which you're not a member. Following a chat room as a non-member does not give you the opportunity to post updates, but is a great feature for monitoring projects that might impact on the activities you are involved with in your own projects.

In this section:

- Changing chat room view
- Creating a new chat room
- Following a chat room
- Creating a new topic feed
- Searching for a chat room

Changing chat room view

The home page for a persistent chat room located within your Lync 2013 client enables you to view rooms according to your relationship to them. For instance, you are able to view the chat rooms you follow, the chat rooms you are members of, or new chat room in which colleagues or coworkers have made you a member. Switching between views is straightforward, as the following demonstrates.

Change chat room view

1 In the Lync client window, click the Persistent Chat button.

2 Click the New tab to see the rooms to which you have recently been added.

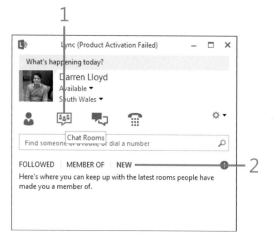

Creating a new chat room

If you have been given permission to do so, Lync 2013 gives you with the ability to create new persistent chat rooms. The type of chat rooms you create is entirely up to you, but often they will be work-related and based on the projects you are involved with or leading. Setting up a chat room for each individual project you are working on will provide a simple environment

in which members of the project team can discuss progress and post questions in the form of instant messages to which they need answers. The point is that persistent chat rooms are designed to speed up access to knowledge and information while simultaneously encouraging awareness and participation.

Create a new chat room

1 In the Lync client window, click the Persistent Chat button.

2 Click the Add button (the plus sign).

3 On the menu that appears, click Create A Chat Room.

(continued on next page)

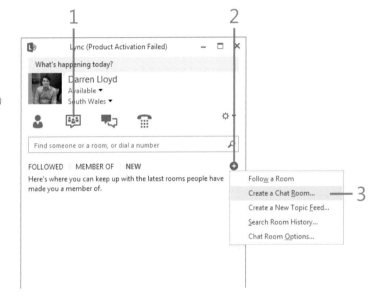

Create a new chat room (continued)

4 On the Manage Persistent Chat Rooms sign-in page, enter your credentials in the Domain\Username and Password text boxes.

5 Click Sign In.

6 On the My Rooms page, click Create A New Room.

7 Type the name of the new chat room.

8 Provide a description of the room.

9 Click the desired privacy level.

10 Insert the first and last name of colleagues and coworkers to whom you want to grant membership of your new chat room. Click the user lookup button to confirm and then click Create.

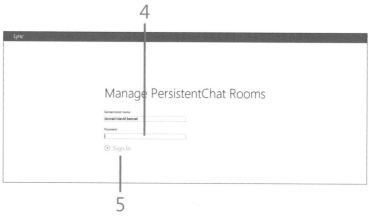

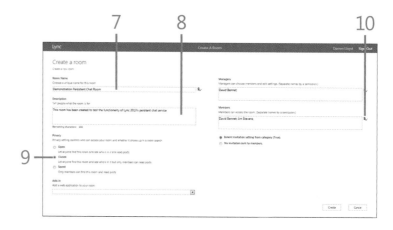

TIP After you've selected the persistent chat button, you can also press Ctrl+R on your keyboard to create a new chat room.

Following a chat room

Your direct involvement in a project might on occasion deter-mine whether you are set up as a member of a particular chat room, and as a consequence, your ability to post updates within that chat room might be restricted. However, it maybe that you're interested in a particular chat room because the proj-ect to which it relates, in some way impacts upon the projects you are dealing with, and therefore the information contained within the room is useful to you. In this scenario, and provided that the chat rooms administrator has allowed you to do so, you might be able to follow a particular chat room. You won't be able to update the room yourself, but you will be able to view and receive notifications when others post updates.

Follow a chat room

1 In the persistent chat search box, type the name of the room that you want to follow.

2 Hover over the room and then select the Add button (the plus sign).

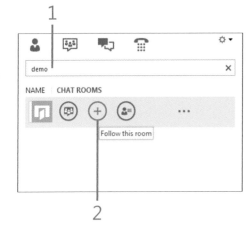

TIP After your search for a persistent chat room has returned its result, you can right-click the room you want and then, on the shortcut menu that appears, click Add to follow the room.

Creating a new topic feed

Topic feeds help you stay up to date with what's going on in the chat rooms in which you are involved or have an interest, without the need to enter the chat room to check for updates. The ability to set up a new topic feed that updates you when specific words or phrases are added is a great time-saving feature that you'll come to appreciate. Topic feeds only relate to the persistent chat rooms you are currently following. They appear in the same tab as the rooms you follow.

The Ego Feed topic feed is created by default; it is set to alert you to any messages that contain your name.

Create new topic feed

1   In the Lync client window, click the Persistent Chat button.

2   Click the Add button (the plus sign).

3   On the menu that appears, click Create A New Topic Feed.

(continued on next page)

Create new topic feed (continued)

4 In the Create A Topic Feed dialog box, enter the name of the topic feed.

5 Type the word(s) about which you want to be notified when they're included within a chat room update, and select how you want for them to be matched.

(continued on next page)

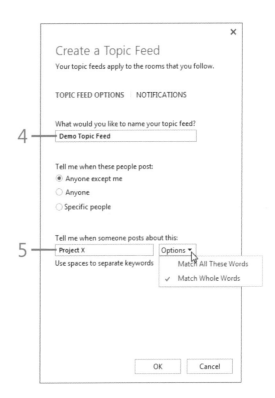

Create new topic feed _(continued)_

6 Click the Notifications tab and configure how you want to be alerted.

7 Click OK.

Searching for persistent chat rooms

Searching for the persistent chat rooms that you want to follow
is a straightforward task in Lync 2013.

Search for a persistent chat room

1 In the Lync client window, click the Persistent Chat button.

2 In the Search box, begin typing the name of the persistent chat
room for which you want to search.

3 Lync 2013 returns all the persistent chat rooms that match the
name as you type it.

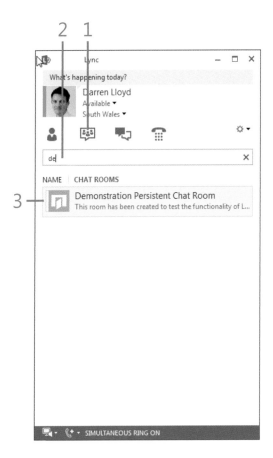

Configuring the Lync options menu

14

Microsoft has approached the world of unified communications from a completely new perspective, and, as a result, it has empowered its users. With Microsoft Lync 2013, users have the power to dictate how and when they communicate, how calls are distributed to colleagues when they are unavailable, and which devices to use when on a telephone or conference call; the tools are available to you from any device with a connection to the Internet.

This change in focus also means that you can do all this without the need to approach your IT staff to help you.

Having been given this ability, it would be a good idea to look at the options available, so in this section, we cover how to change your picture, how to change your ringtones for specific call types, how to select different audio/video devices, and even how to add additional phone numbers by which your contacts can reach you.

Like most things in Lync, the Options dialog box is straightforward and intuitive to use, and I encourage you to spend some time editing the settings until you have a communications environment that caters to your individual needs.

Configuring the General options

The General tab in the Lync 2013 Options dialog box is where you can configure how your instant message windows are displayed, giving you the option, if you so choose, to have them displayed in a tabbed window as opposed to each instant message session having an individual window of its own.

Additionally, the General tab is where you can configure Lync to collate stats relating to the features that you use most frequently. It's also where you can see how your system is configured. This information can then be sent to Microsoft to help it improve the product.

Configure the General options

1   In the Lync client window, click the Settings button.

2   In the Options dialog box, click the General tab.

3   View the options that you can edit.

Note the three separate categories: Conversation Window, Help Us Improve, and Help Your Support Team Help You.

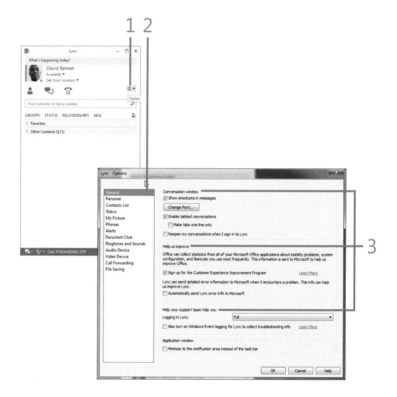

Modifying the Personal options

The Personal tab in the Lync 2013 Options dialog box is where you can modify the settings associated with the amount of information you provide others when they view your contact card. On the Personal tab, you can decide whether to share subject and location information about the meetings you attend, configure whether to update your presence information based

upon entries within you Outlook calendar, show your picture, and even choose whether to save IM conversations as emails within your Outlook Conversation History folder.

The Personal tab is also where you can change your Lync 2013 sign-in credentials.

Modify your Personal options

1 In the Lync client window, click the Settings button.

2 In the Options dialog box, click the Personal tab.

3 View the options that you can edit.

Note the four separate categories: My Account, Personal Information Manager, Location, and Show Pictures.

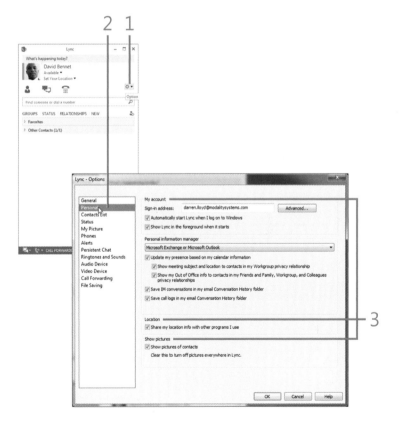

Changing the Contacts List options

The Contacts List tab in the Lync 2013 Options dialog box is where you configure how to view your contacts within the Lync client. You can choose whether to include pictures of your contacts and whether you view your contacts by name or availability. You can also select other options such as whether to include the Favorites group.

Change the Contacts List options

1 In the Lync client window, click the Settings button.

2 In the Options dialog box, click the Contacts List tab.

3 View the options that you can edit.

   Note the three separate categories: Display My Contacts With, Order My List, and Show This Information.

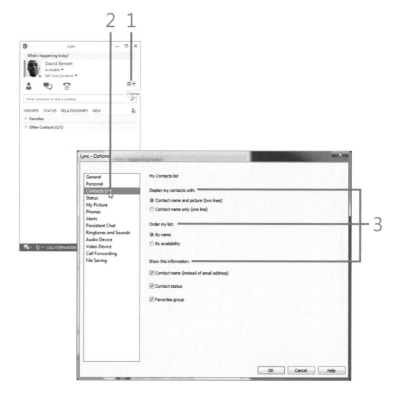

Setting the Status options

The Status tab in the Lync 2013 Options dialog box is where you configure how and when your status changes automatically. You can configure the length of time for which your computer can be idle before your presence automatically changes to Inactive. You can change the amount of time that passes before your

presence automatically changes from Inactive to Away. You can also choose how and when your presence is automatically set to Do Not Disturb, for example, when you are presenting your desktop or when your monitor is duplicated.

Set the Status options

1 In the Lync client window, click the Settings button.

2 In the Options dialog box, click the Status tab.

3 View the options that you can edit.

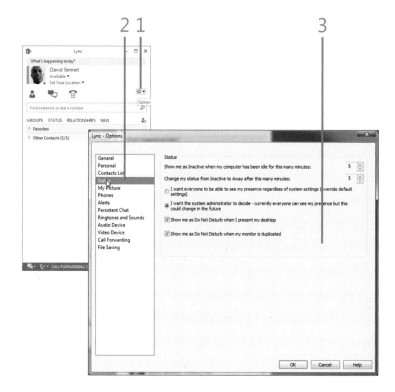

Modifying the My Picture options

The My Picture tab in the Lync 2013 Options dialog box is where you can make changes to the way your picture is displayed when others view your contact card. From within this menu, you are able to select whether to display your picture and also, providing that your administrator has allowed you to do so, select the picture that you want to display.

Change the My Picture options

1   In the Lync client window, click the Settings button.

2   In the Options dialog box, click the My Picture tab.

3   View the options that you can edit.

Configuring the Phones options

The Phone tab in the Lync 2013 Options dialog box is where you can add additional numbers that you want to display on your contact card. Depending on how your administrator has configured Lync, your work and mobile phone number might already

be included, but you have the option of including your home number, plus one additional number. You can also configure the default number from which you join the conference calls you have scheduled.

Configure the Phones options

1 In the Lync client window, click the Settings button.

2 In the Options dialog box, click the Phones tab.

3 View the options that you can edit.

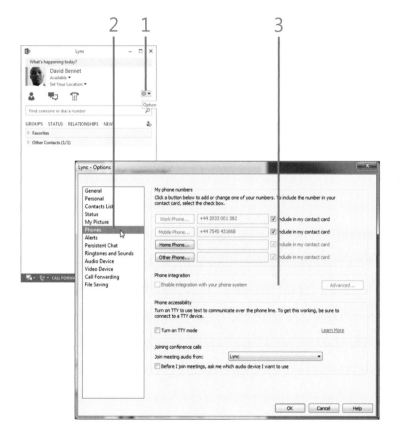

Modifying the Alerts options

The Alerts tab in the Lync 2013 Options dialog box is where you configure how you are alerted by Lync to particular activities. The alerts tab includes the ability to turn on/off notifications to inform you that you have been added to someone's contact list and also to configure the types of alerts you receive when your presence is set to Do Not Disturb. Additionally, you can configure alerts to notify you of instances when individuals who do not use Lync (they instead use other external IM applications) attempt to add you to their contact list.

Change the Alerts options

1   In the Lync client window, click the Settings button.

2   In the Options dialog box, click the Alerts tab.

3   View the options that you can edit.

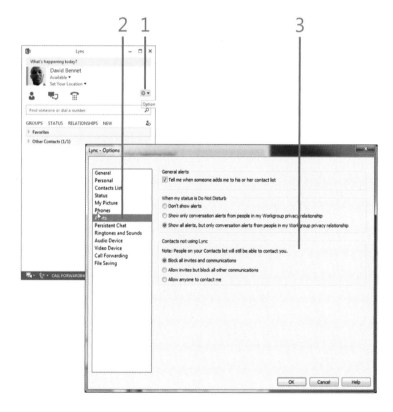

Changing the Persistent Chat options

The Persistent Chat tab in the Lync 2013 Options dialog box is where you personalize your chat rooms and configure how you are informed of updates to your chat rooms and topic feeds. On the Persistent Chat menu, you can configure Lync to display a message informing you of an update in a new window or, if you would prefer, configure it to play a sound. You can also set alerts for both new messages and messages marked as high importance.

Change the Persistent Chat options

1   In the Lync client window, click the Settings button.

2   In the Options dialog box, click the Persistent Chat tab.

3   View the options that you can edit.

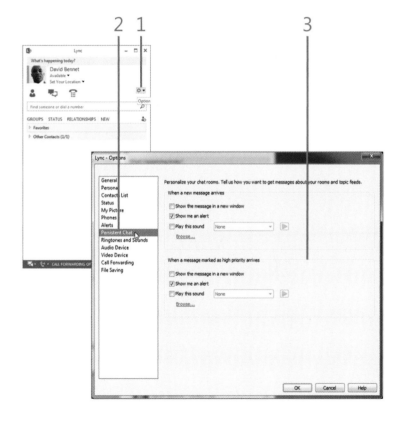

Editing the Ringtones And Sounds options

The Ringtone And Sounds tab in the Lync 2013 Options dialog box is where you can configure different ringtones for different types of incoming calls. For example, you can set different ringtones for incoming calls to your work number, your team-call groups, individuals for whom you are set up as a delegate, and also for the response groups of which you are a member. Additionally, you can also configure whether to disable sounds when your presence is set to Busy or Do Not Disturb.

Edit the Ringtones And Sounds options

1 In the Lync client window, click the Settings button.

2 In the Options dialog box, click the Ringtones And Sounds tab.

3 View the options that you can edit.

   Note the two separate categories: Ringtones and Sounds.

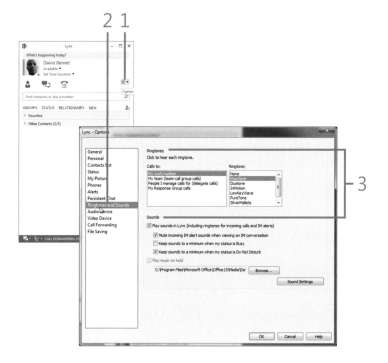

Modifying the Audio Device options

The Audio Device tab in the Lync 2013 Options dialog box is where you can edit the settings associated with your audio device; for example, your headset or desk phone. Options to change the default volume settings of your speaker, microphone, and ringer are provided, together with the ability to configure a secondary device that will also ring. This is a particularly useful feature when you have a headset configured as your primary device but need your laptop speakers to handle the incoming call. One other useful feature found on the Audio Device tab is the ability to make a test call to see how you sound to others when using a particular device.

Modify the Audio Device options

1 In the Lync client window, click the Settings button.

2 In the Options dialog box, click the Audio Device tab.

3 View the options that you can edit.

Note the three separate categories: Audio Device, Secondary Ringer, and Stereo Audio Playback.

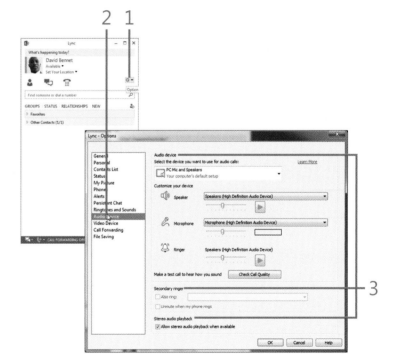

Setting the Video Device options

The Video Device tab in the Lync 2013 Options dialog box is where you can edit the settings of your video device. On this tab, you can switch between integrated or external webcams, view how you look, and also modify specific webcam settings.

Set the Video Device options

1 In the Lync client window, click the Settings button.

2 In the Options dialog box, click the Video Device tab.

3 View the options that you can edit.

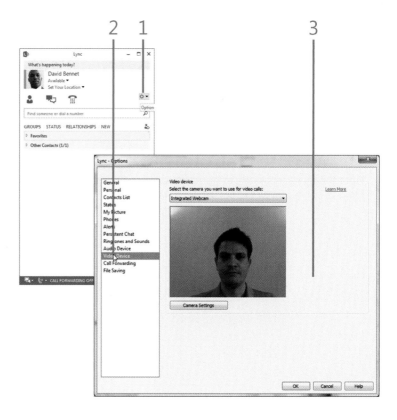

Configuring the Call Forwarding options

The Call Forwarding tab in the Lync 2013 Options dialog box is where you manage your incoming call environment. On this menu you are able to set up call forwarding rules and edit your simultaneous ring settings so that incoming calls will also ring other team members, your mobile, or any other number that you want to include. The Call Forwarding tab also provides a dedicated area that informs you of your current call forwarding or simultaneous ring settings. Here, you can configure options that dictate what happens to a call that remains unanswered after a set period of time.

Configure the Call Forwarding options

1 In the Lync client window, click the Settings button.

2 In the Options dialog box, click the Call Forwarding tab.

3 View the options that you can edit.

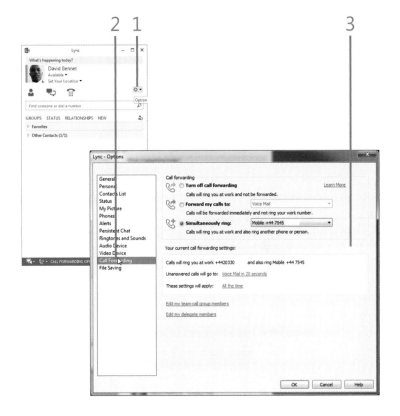

Changing the File Saving options

The File Saving tab in the Lync 2013 Options dialog box is where you can edit the folders to which your Lync 2013 shared files and recordings are stored. The files saved are those sent from within the instant message window, and the recordings are those of the online meetings you have attended and have opted to record.

Change the File Saving options

1 In the Lync client window, click the Settings button.

2 In the Options dialog box, click the File Saving tab.

3 View the options that you can edit.

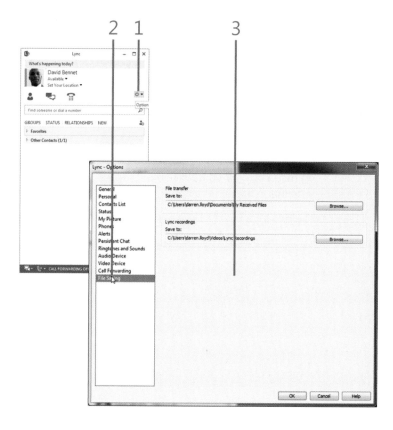

Microsoft Lync keyboard shortcuts

As you become more proficient in navigating and using the multitude of features available in Lync 2013, you may wish to improve the speed by which you access some of these features and save even more of your valuable time, by utilizing the keyboard shortcuts made available to you.

The following pages contain over 100 keyboard shortcuts, all provided with the goal of improving and simplifying the way you are able to navigate Lync 2013 and its feature set.

Table A-1 General (any window) no matter which window has the focus

Press this key or keyboard shortcut	To do this
Windows logo key+A	Accept an incoming invite notification.
Windows logo key+Esc	Decline an invite notification.
Windows logo key+Y	Open the main window and put focus in the Search box.
Windows logo key+F4	Self-mute/unmute audio.
Windows logo key+F5	Turn my Camera On/Turn my Camera Off when video is already established in the call.
Ctrl+Shift+Spacebar	Put focus on the application sharing toolbar.
Ctrl+Alt+Spacebar	Take back control when sharing your screen.
Ctrl+Shift+S	Stop sharing your screen.

Table A-2 Lync main window when it's in the foreground

Press this key or keyboard shortcut	To do this
Ctrl+1	Move to the Contacts list tab.
Ctrl+2	Move to the persistent chat tab.
Ctrl+3	Move to the Conversation list tab.
Ctrl+4	Move to the Phone tab.
Ctrl+1 or Ctrl+Shift+1	As a delegate, transfer a call to someone else's work number. (Not available in Lync Basic or with all Office 365 subscriptions.)
Alt+Spacebar	Open the System menu. Alt opens the menu bar.
Alt+F	Open the File menu.

Press this key or keyboard shortcut	To do this
Alt+M	Start Meet Now.
Alt+T	Open the Tools menu.
Alt+H	Open the Help menu.

Table A-3   Contacts list

Press this key or keyboard shortcut	To do this
Delete	Delete the selected custom group or contact.
Alt+Up Arrow	Move the selected group up.
Alt+Down Arrow	Move the selected group down.
Alt+Enter	On the shortcuts menu—open the selected contact or group contacts card.
Spacebar	Collapse or expand the selected group.
Shift+Delete	Remove the selected contact from the Contacts list (non-distribution-group members only).

Table A-4   Contact card

Press this key or keyboard shortcut	To do this
Esc	Close the contact card.
Ctrl+Tab	Move through the tabs at the bottom of the contact card.
Ctrl+Shift+Tab	Move through the tabs at the bottom of the contact card in reverse order.
Alt+Enter	Open a contact card.

Table A-5   Conversation window

Press this key or keyboard shortcut	To do this
F1	Open the Help home page (on the Help menu).
Esc	Exit full-screen view if present. Otherwise, the Conversation window closes only if there is no audio, video, or sharing occurring.
Alt+C	Accept any of the invite notifications. These include audio, video, call, and sharing requests.
Alt+F4	Close the Conversation window.
Alt+I	Ignore any invite notifications. These include audio, video, call, and sharing requests.
Alt+R	Rejoin audio in a meeting.
Alt+S	Open the Save As dialog box for a file that was sent in the Conversation window.
Alt+V	Invite a contact to an existing conversation.
Ctrl+S	Save the contents of IM history. Works for person-to-person conversations when you use Outlook.
Ctrl+W	Show or hide the instant message area.
Ctrl+F	Send a file, or in the context of a conference, add a meeting attachment.
Ctrl+N	Take your own notes by using Microsoft OneNote. Starts OneNote. (Not available in Lync Basic.)
Ctrl+R	Show or hide the participant list.
Ctrl+Shift+Enter	Add video/end video.
Ctrl+Shift+H	Hold or resume an ongoing audio conversation.
Ctrl+Shift+I	Mark a conversation as having high importance. Works for person-to-person conversations, but isn't available for meetings.

Press this key or keyboard shortcut	To do this
Ctrl+Shift+Y	Show or hide the sharing stage.
Ctrl+Shift+P	Switch to compact view.
Ctrl+Shift+K	Switch to content-only view.
Ctrl+Enter	Add audio/end audio.
Up Arrow	When on a mode button, opens the corresponding callout.
Spacebar	When focus is on a mode button, a default action is taken. So, for audio, mute or unmute occurs, whereas for video, it starts or stops the camera.
Esc	Dismiss or hide an open callout or bubble that has keyboard focus.

The persistent chat window uses the same shortcuts as the conversation window.

Table A-6 Call controls (in the Conversation window) while in a peer-to-peer call

Press this keyboard shortcut	To do this
Alt+Q	End a call.
Ctrl+Shift+T	Transfer: Open the contact picker during a peer-to-peer call. (Not available in Lync Basic or with all Office 365 subscriptions.)
Ctrl+Shift+H	Put a call on hold.
Ctrl+Shift+D	Display the dial pad.

These shortcuts do not work in a conference call.

Table A-7   Video (in the Conversation window)

Press this key or keyboard shortcut	To do this
F5	View video in full screen. If the stage area is visible in the Conversation window, F5 won't take full-screen video.
Esc	Exit full-screen video.
Ctrl+Shift+O	Pop out Gallery; Pop in Gallery.
Ctrl+Shift+L	Lock your video for everyone in the meeting.

Table A-8   IM (in the Conversation window)

Press this key or keyboard shortcut	To do this
F1	Open Help.
F12	Save the IM conversation.
Shift+Enter	Add carriage returns.
Shift+Insert or Ctrl+V	Paste.
Ctrl+A	Select all content.
Ctrl+B	Make the selected text bold.
Ctrl+C	Copy the selected text.
Ctrl+X	Cut the selected text.
Ctrl+I	Italicize the selected text.
Ctrl+U	Underline the selected text.
Ctrl+Y	Redo the last action.

Press this key or keyboard shortcut	To do this
Ctrl+Z	Undo the last action.
Ctrl+Shift+F	Change the color of the font. (Only changes color for what you type, not for what the other person types.)
Alt+P	Open a file that's been received.
Alt+D	Decline a file that's been sent.

The persistent chat window uses the same shortcuts as IM.

Table A-9   Conversation or meeting stage

Press this key or keyboard shortcut	To do this
F5	View the Conversation window meeting stage in full screen.
Esc	Exit full screen if present.
Alt+T	Stop sharing.
Ctrl+Shift+E	Manage presentable content.
Ctrl+Shift+Y	Show or hide the sharing stage.
Ctrl+Shift+A	Force pending L1 alert into view in full screen.
Ctrl+Shift+J	Switch to speaker view.
Ctrl+Shift+I	Switch to gallery view.
Ctrl+Shift+Right Arrow or Ctrl+Shift+Left Arrow	Tab out of the sharing region in a forward direction, and/or tab out of the sharing region in a backward direction.

Table A-10   Conversation environment

Press this key or keyboard shortcut	To do this
Delete	Delete selected items.
Home	Move top of list.
End	Move to bottom of list.
Page Up	Move one page up.
Page Down	Move one page down.
Up Arrow	Move up to the previous contact for conversation.
Down Arrow	Move down to the next contact for conversation.

Table A-11   PPT sharing: Legacy PPT viewer

Press this key or keyboard shortcut	To do this
Tab	When the content space is in focus, tab through the controls for PPT sharing (Prev arrow, Next arrow, Thumbnails, and Notes).
Right Arrow	When focus is on content area, move to the next click, or slide, if no click for animation is on the current slide.
Left or Right Arrow	When the thumbnail area is in focus, move focus to the previous or next thumbnail without changing the active slide.
Left Arrow	When focus is on content area, move to the previous click, or slide if no click for animation is on the current slide.
Home	When thumbnail area is in focus, set the focus on the first slide thumbnail without changing the active slide.

Press this key or keyboard shortcut	To do this
Enter	Select the control in focus or thumbnails if thumbnail strip has focus and select (change in active slide).
End	When the thumbnail area is in focus, set the focus on the last slide thumbnail without changing the active slide.

Table A-12   Tabbed conversations

Press this key or keyboard shortcut	To do this
Alt+Spacebar	Open tab window's system menu.
Ctrl+Shift+T	Set focus on tab item in tabbed conversation view.
Ctrl+Tab	Switch to the next tab (continuously loop through all tabs).
Ctrl+1,2...9	Switch to a specific tab number and put keyboard focus in that conversation. Ctrl+1.
Ctrl+O	Undock/dock the selected conversation from/to the tab window.
Esc	Close a tab.

Index

End key, 198, 199
Enter key, 199
escalating conversations to video or voice
    call, 66
Esc key, 193–197, 199
Exchange auto attendant, 138
external contacts
    adding to group, 44
    presence for, 44

F

F1 key, 194, 196
F5 key, 196–197
F12 key, 196
Favorites group, 42
files
    blocked types, 63
    in conversations
        receiving, 65
        sending, 63–64
File Saving tab, 190
Folder pane, Outlook, 102, 148
following persistent chats, 171
fonts, changing, 54–55
forwarding calls
    settings for, 122–123
    to voicemail, 101
forwarding voicemails, 148–149
Forward My Calls To option, 123
Frequent Contacts group, 42

G

Gallery view, 14
General tab, Options dialog box, 178
greetings, voicemail, 146–147
groups, contact
    adding external contact to, 44
    adding internal contact to, 42–43

creating, 40–41
removing from, 45–46
viewing in Microsoft Outlook, 95
Groups tab, 31, 40

H

Help Us improve category, 178
Help Your Support Team Help You
    category, 178
hiding conversations, 56
"high importance" conversations, 52–53
history
    of conversations, 33
    viewing in Microsoft Outlook, 88
Hold Call option, 103
on hold, placing calls, 103
Home key, 198
Home page, Lync Web App, 94
Home tab, Microsoft Outlook, 76, 87

I

Ignore option, Incoming Call pop-up
    notification, 101
"I'll be late" notification, 144–145
IM (instant message)
    button for, 50, 60
    changing font, 54–55
    defined, 49
    escalating to voice or video call, 66
    hiding area of window, 56
    implications of, 50
    inviting additional contacts to, 57–58
    marking as "high importance", 52–53
    receiving files in, 65
    responding to email using, 84
    sending, 50–51
    sending files in, 63–64

tabs in
    closing, 62
    creating, 59–60
    overview, 9
    popping to separate window, 61
In a Conference Call presence, 83
In a meeting presence, 83
Include In My Contact Card check box, 113
Incoming Call notification, 100–101, 116
incoming calls, 100
indicators, presence status, 27
instant message (IM). *See* IM
internal contacts, 42–43
Invite By Email option, 159
inviting contacts to conversation, 57–58
italics, 54

J

Join By Phone number, 155
joining online meetings
    via Lync 2013 client, 154
    via mobile phone, 155
    overview, 78–79
Join Lync Meeting option, Outlook, 93
Join Online button, Outlook, 80
Join Online Meeting option, Outlook, 154

K

keyboard shortcuts, 191–199

L

Left Arrow key, 198
Location category, 179
location for presence status, 29
Lync client window, 21
Lync Meeting group, Outlook, 152, 157
Lync Meeting Options dialog box, 157

About the author

Darren Lloyd has worked in the IT industry for nearly 20 years, learning his trade as a technician and moving through the ranks into positions where he's been responsible for managing large IT and communications departments.

He obtained an MSc in technology management from the University of Wales, writing his dissertation on the "Impact of Unified Communications in the Contact Center." He has presented at numerous unified communications events, including the launch of Microsoft Lync in the United Kingdom.

More recently, he has taken the knowledge that he's gained while managing IT departments and deploying Microsoft Lync, and via his position within Modality Systems, now advises global organizations on how Lync can impact the delivery of corporate strategies while improving communication and productivity within the workplace.